LEAD GUITAR WORKSHOP

Lead Guitar: Chords+Arpeggios

L.&.W
LEAD GUITAR WORKSHOP

Library of Congress Control Number:

Any references to historical events, real people, or real places are used fictitiously. Names, characters, and places are products of the author's imagination.

Front cover image by Suke Cerulo
Book design by Suke Cerulo
Front Cover by Jessical Macelli
Inside/Back cover photo: Paul Citone
About Author Photo by Paul Citone
Student Reviewer Linda Ameroso

Printed by Lead Guitar Workshop, Inc., in the United States of America.

First edition 2021.

SCAN FOR MORE

for all backing tracks and videos

www.LeadGuitarWorkshop.com

PREFACE

I always enjoyed music as a kid but my immediate family was not musical. There wasn't a lot of music playing in the house and we were never the type of family to sing. But my Grandfather George Lane was a Big Band musician and bandleader in the 1950's in Boston and New York. I don't have any memories of him playing music but he would have hilarious stories "from the road" traveling with the band. Later in life I really learned to appreciate them as I toured extensively.

It was 1984 and I heard Van Halen for the first time. I knew right then and there that I wanted to play music. I got my first guitar for Christmas in that year and quickly took lessons because I had no idea what to do. At the time I was really into playing football and I was good at it. I realized I was never going to be in the NFL or make a career out of it. But I did realize there was no NFL of music, anybody could play! That was so exciting. I knew I was going to play music for my whole life. I just had to figure out how to make it a career.

I had weekly guitar lessons from the time I was twelve until I graduated High School. For most of this time my teacher was Sandy Prager. He played "third stream jazz" on a nylon string guitar. This was as far away from Van Halen as possible without being a classical guitarist. But I learned so much about music, how to think about it and improvise. He constantly had me creating. Once I finished High School I went to **Berklee College of Music**. It was the only school I wanted to go to. After four years I got my Bachelors Degree in Professional Music.

My one goal upon graduating was to join a band. Fortunately for me I met my future bandmates of 30 plus years. We formed the band "**Schleigho**" in 1993 and toured full time within a year or so. We toured 200 plus dates a year for almost five years straight and still play to this day. We recorded and released 5 albums. We signed a label with the **Allman Brothers Band**, toured with **Derek Trucks,** and played with so very many people all over the country. This was my "real world" music education.

But even though I had lessons in High School and a great experience at Berklee I still felt like I was slow learning and still really didn't get the true nature of music and guitar. I struggled to connect the musical dots.

I had to build confidence to make my own conclusions about music. I heard so many different ideas, terms, explanations and they were confusing. I was perplexed that music had been around for hundreds of years and there was still so much indecision about ideas and terminology.

I had to separate music from the instrument. This was one of my biggest realizations. It came into fruition when I started playing flute. I realized the music was its own language independent of the instrument that plays it. When I started really practicing flute my guitar playing got better! I was stunned, but I realized my musicianship was better and it was now translating to guitar.

Once my band started touring I had guitar players (and flute players) asking me for lessons. I think I gave my first lesson in 1995. It was very casual and it was new to me but I was just trying to help people out. I realized I had a good way of explaining things and I was able to connect with people. Over the years I kept teaching. It was rewarding and I was learning a lot by having to explain music to people in many different ways.

About six months after I moved to NYC in 2003 I got my first real teaching job at a guitar school in NYC. I was touring and teaching full time. I was engulfed in playing and teaching music and it was wonderful. As touring slowed down the teaching picked up. I was teaching ten classes and about thirty private students. Close to eighty folks a week were coming to see me to learn about guitar and music. After years of teaching groups and private students I was able to refine my approach to teaching and to understanding music and how it relates to the guitar. Years ago I estimated that I hit my 10,000 hours as a guitar player. Now I was hitting my 10,000 hours as a teacher.

In 2003 I wrote my first book "Lead Guitar Basics" for me to use at the guitar school. Over the years this grew into five complete books and a number of rewrites. I also became the Director of the Lead Guitar Department. I train other teachers to teach my material and musically evaluate all incoming teachers to the school.

I was amassing an unprecedented amount of teaching experience and gaining access to hundreds, if not thousands, of guitar players struggling in the same way I had. Over years of refinement I was able to develop this entire pedagogy for learning lead guitar.

These books have three decades of experience behind them and seventeen years of in-classroom development. I believe in these books, and I think they will help you immensely as you become a better guitarist and musician. These are all the things I wish I had when I was starting my journey.

HOW TO USE BOOK

Each book is written as ten lessons continually building on each other. The books all work together and are meant to extend and expand your knowledge as you work and grow with them. Go through them in order and go back later to revisit topics.

These books were initially created as 10 week courses, one chapter per week. You can use it in the same way. Each Chapter is about an hour long. There are enough warm-ups, exercises, new skills and practice to last you for a week. There is overlap and repetition in the books to really help reinforce the core ideas.

Every lesson is structured the same way. It is meant to optimize your learning, efficiency, and time. The repetition creates good habits.

Tune in: First you have to get in the right head space. You must remind yourself that you are a musician and a guitar player. That music is Melody, Harmony, and Rhythm; and that rhythm is the number one factor to sounding good. It's like a mantra.

Warm-up: These are exercises to get your musical blood flowing and synchronize your internal clock. There are usually up to three warm-ups; *Muted String Ladders*, *Shells*, and *Changing Gears*. They are all music based and are like push-ups and jumping jacks to athletes.

Exercises: These are straight up music exercises like scales, arpeggios and more.

Review: This is part of the learning circle. You must review everything you learn. Eventually that will become part of your everyday language.

New Topic: Learn something new. It can be big or small, but it should expand your knowledge, even if it's learning something new about something you already know.

Practice: Play! Get better by playing music. Use your new idea/technique, concept in real time in the music you are playing, even if it is a one chord jam by yourself. Self Generating music and backing tracks are a focal point.

Summary: A reminder of what has been learned so far. Summaries compound with each chapter.

Going through each word and each note as written in these books is only part of the bigger picture. You have to imagine how music is working and how it relates to your instrument. You have to have a desire to grow and a never ending curiosity about music. If you keep questioning music you will find more answers and go deeper and deeper. You have to "drive" music, start a song yourself, jam on it and make it music all by yourself. When you're playing by yourself and someone walks in they should ask you "What song are you playing?" not "What are you practicing?" Learning music and playing is not about checking off a list of requirements. It's about sounding like a musician playing good music, and not someone noodling at the guitar store.

At a certain point in your musical life, you will learn all the information about music that you will ever use. Then your growth is about becoming closer to that information and growing deeper with it every time you revisit it. There isn't a learning path in music, it's a learning circle. An ever expanding circle is like rings in a tree. It's the growth in the rings, in the trunk of the tree that allows those branches to grow and extend.

Music is just a language and a guitar is just an instrument. Both are silent without you, you are music!

As guitarists Pat Martino and Mike Stern both told me, and I will tell you, "Just keep playing." Enjoy!

Suke Cerulo

Table of Contents

Lead Guitar – Chords + Arpeggios

This book is for advanced lead guitar players who are comfortable using pentatonic and mode scales in different keys. This is for the player who wants to expand their musical knowledge of notes in chords and on the fretboard, and use them as arpeggios, chord inversions, guide tones, and more. This book is for those wanting to rely on notes and knowledge more than black dot diagrams. If your thinking "what finger, what string, what fret?" this is for you. This book focuses on using arpeggios as a melodic tool for solos, compared to the rhythm guitar of fingerpicking.

CHAPTER 1

TUNE IN

"I am a musician and a guitar player. Music is my language and my guitar is my voice. Music is Melody, Harmony and Rhythm. I develop my language skills and my instrument skills. They are two separate worlds working together to complete the circle of music."

Rhythm is the number one factor to sounding great as a musician.

ARPEGGIO

Traditionally an Arpeggio is when the notes of a chord are played in succession, one after another instead of simultaneously. This is usually used for Harmony (accompaniment) but also has its place in melodies.

For guitar players the use of arpeggios falls into two main departments, **POLYPHONIC** and **MONOPHONIC**.

A **polyphonic** arpeggio means the notes are overlapping each other in a sustained manner. This is like the true meaning of the word, like a HARP. We do this on guitar whenever we hold a chord and use a pick (or more often fingerpicking) to pluck the strings individually while all of the notes ring together, sustaining. This would be impossible to sing by one person.

Polyphonic arpeggios fall into the HARMONY side of music. (Think "Dust in the Wind.") This is where "fingerstylists" spend a lot of time. They are holding chords and separating the notes in lieu of strumming, playing rhythm guitar. As a guitar player this is the whole world of FINGERPICKING.

A **monophonic** arpeggio is something we could sing, literally, one note-at-a-time going up and back over the notes in the chord. We do this as a method for soloing.

The **monophonic** arpeggios are in the MELODY. For us this can translate into repeated single note arpeggios in solos. (Think the second half of the guitar solo in "Hotel California" or the end of the solo in "Sultans of Swing.")

Here is an example of both types of arpeggios: Polyphonic and Monophonic

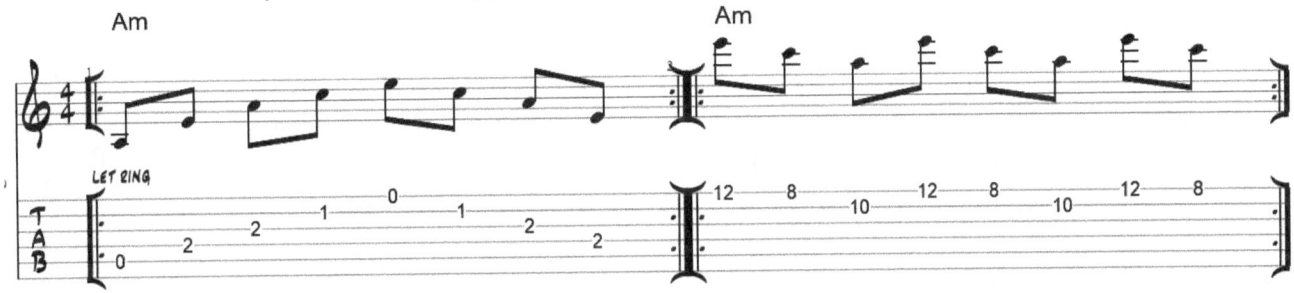

An arpeggio only contains CHORD TONES (the notes in the chord). When played in a repeated fashion they create a very unique sound and a great alternative to the blues "call and response" style of music.

IMPORTANT: Knowing the chord tones is extremely valuable as you can use them in other ways beyond the repeated fashion they usually occur. Chord tones can connect musical lines like fence posts. It will help establish the chords sound without sounding like lots of repeating notes. You can see the chord tones in your scale patterns to help you use the pattern based approach more musically.

WARM UP

Muted String Ladder 3 Strings
All 4 gears PICKED: All UP, All DOWN, and All ALTERNATE

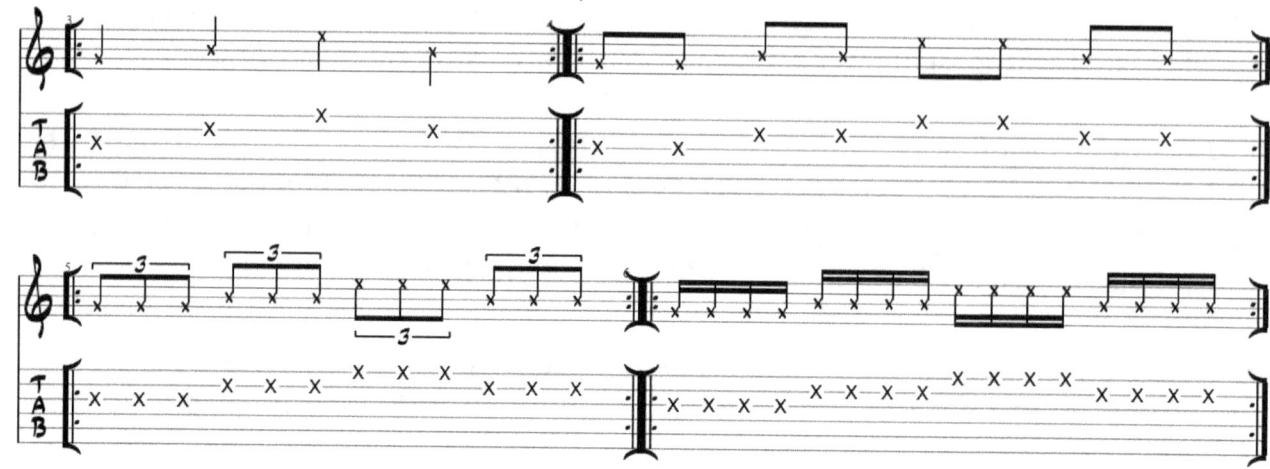

SHELL 1 4 (minor 3rd) eighth-notes

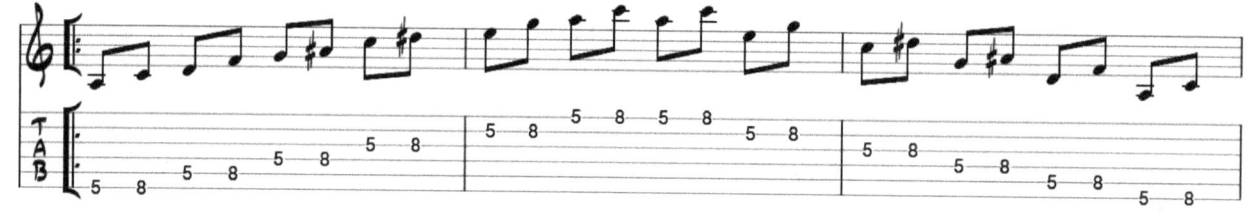

SHELL STRETCH 1 4 (Major 3rd) eighth-notes

THINKING CHORDS

One of the hardest parts about playing arpeggios is keeping the chord progression in your head as you are soloing (also true when "playing the changes"). *This is extremely important for any musician.* You have to know where you are in a chord progression at all times. This is an essential musical skill.

MUSICAL TRUTHS

The first step is to know the notes as a musician.

Think like a musician first. Here are a few MUSICAL TRUTHS:

- There are 12 notes in all of music. Seven of them are A B C D E F G known as the "natural" notes.

- A Half-step (H) in music is the smallest distance between notes (1 fret).

- A Whole-step (W) is two half-steps (2 frets).

- Sharp (#) raises a note/chord/scale by a half-step.

- Flat (*b*) lowers a note/chord/scale by half-step.

- Sharped and flat notes are know as "accidentals" and they have two names. For example F# is also G*b*.

- There are 7 Natural notes and 5 Accidentals to make 12 total notes.

- All notes are a whole-step apart (2 frets) except BC and EF which are half-steps (1 fret) (true with open strings too).

- The 12 notes are always in the same order going up and down (especially true on any/all guitar strings).

NATURAL NOTES ON FRETBOARD

The second step is to know the notes on the fretboard for when we need them as a musician. It is easier to start with the natural notes and adjust for sharps and flats later. Don't forget the power of knowing OCTAVE shapes. Use the LONG Octave shape to connect notes of the HIGH E string to the G string.

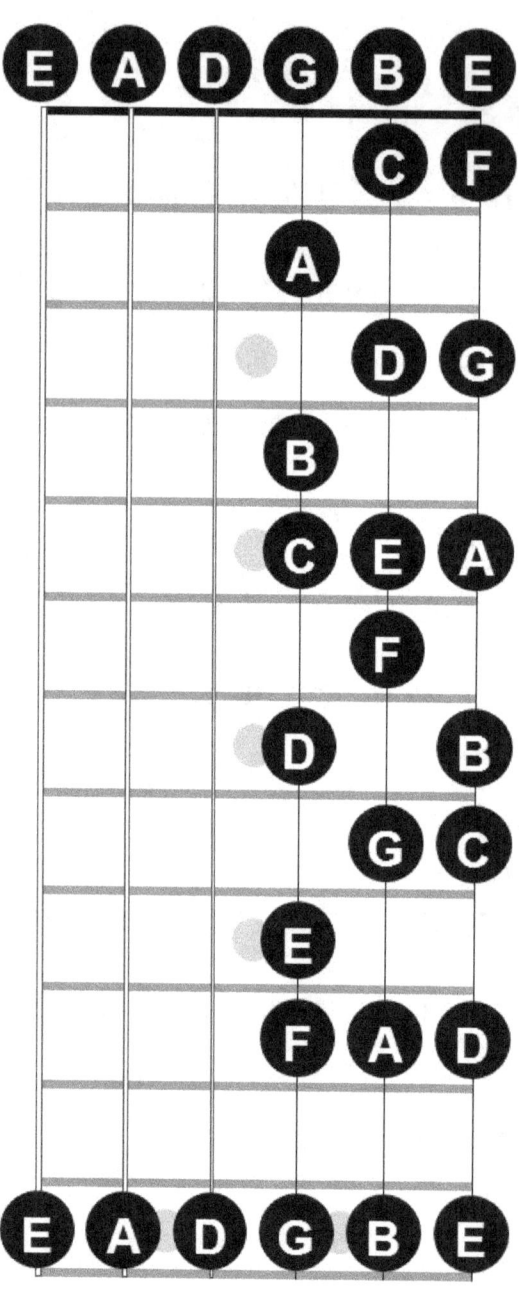
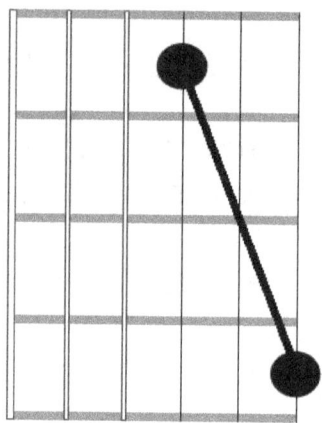

EXERCISE

Ascend and descend EACH string and name every NATURAL note.
Do this for the high E string, the B string and the G string.
Play as quarter-notes at 60 BPM

MELODIC BASS LINES

This is a term I use to describe the first step of playing the changes and arpeggios. The main job for a bass player is to play the root of a chord (root is the first and main note of a chord/scale/arpeggio). They play the root on the downbeat of every chord change and match them to all the chords.

We are going to think like a bass player and play the root note on every chord change. Except, we are going to do it as a melodic idea, and play them in the high register (higher sounding strings). Do this for E, B and G STRINGS. Start with single strings each and then try to mix and match strings.

Follow-Along BACKING TRACK VIDEO

www.LeadGuitarWorkshop

THIRDS

The third in music is very special. It is the "toggle switch" between ANYTHING Major and minor in the music world. This is true for all chords and all scales. If there is no third of a chord/scale then it is neither Major nor minor (for example sus chords or power chords).

In the true sense the third is an interval (distance) between two notes/chords. There are two types:

__Major third__: 2 whole-steps (4 frets from root on any 1 string)

__minor third__: 1 ½ steps (1 whole-step +1 half-step) (3 frets on any 1 string)

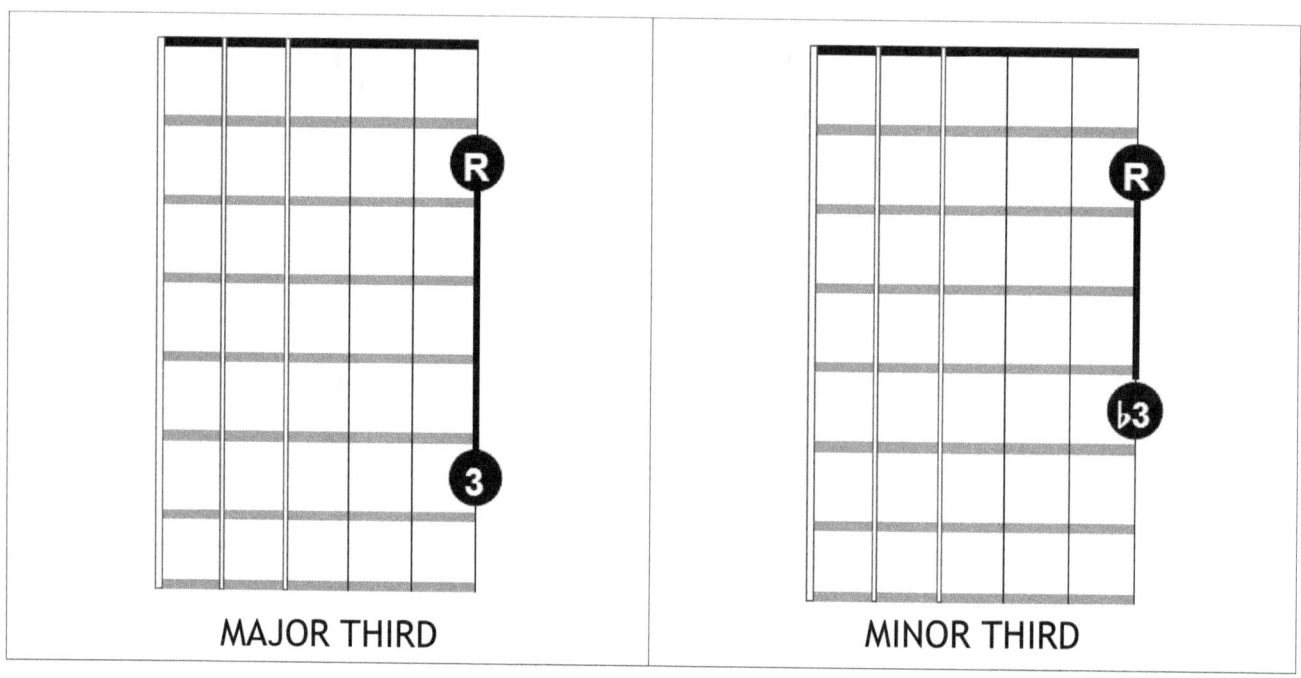

| MAJOR THIRD | MINOR THIRD |

The Third is the "toggle switch" when it starts from the ROOT. Whatever string you are on, the THIRD will always be above the ROOT on the same string, 3 or 4 frets depending upon whether it is a Major or minor chord/scale.

PRACTICE

Here is the same backing track and TAB showing ROOT to THIRDS for each chord using half-notes. It's tabbed on the top 3 strings.

EASY AS 1 2 3

Knowing the first 3 notes of a scale is extremely valuable. Start with the ROOT of the chord. Then move to its THIRD. The note in between is the second, a note with great color and many uses.

EVERY Major scale starts with 1 2 3 (two whole-steps, Do Re Me). This is true for the Major pentatonic, and all 3 Major modes (Ionian, Lydian, Mixolydian).

Minor scales start with 1 2 *b3* (whole-step, then half-step) for Dorian and Aeolian. Flip the intervals to 1 *b2 b3* for Phyrgian. You can also add the 2nd in the minor pentatonic, it adds a great color.

SUMMARY

We are musicians and we are guitar players.

Music is Melody, Harmony, and Rhythm.

We think like a musician first and then go to our instrument.

We must always know the chords in our heads as we play.

Learn to play the ROOT note on every chord change.

THIRDS are the "Toggle Switch" in music, dictating what is Major and what is minor.

Knowing the 1 2 3 of a scale is extremely valuable. It's three of the five notes of a pentatonic scale and three of seven notes of the Mode scales.

Break free from "what finger, what fret, what string?" and simply start looking for the notes.

We will learn the sounds of the intervals of chords. (How does the ROOT sound versus the THIRD when soloing.)

CHAPTER 2

TUNE IN

"I am a musician and a guitar player. Music is my language and my guitar is my voice. Music is Melody, Harmony and Rhythm. I develop my language skills and my instrument skills. They are two separate worlds working together to complete the circle of music."

Rhythm is the number one factor to sounding great as a musician.

WARM UP

Muted String Ladder (MSL) 4 Strings all 4 gears

ALL with *DOWN pick only*, *UP picks only*, and *ALTERNATE pick.*

Do All 3 pickings before changing rhythm.

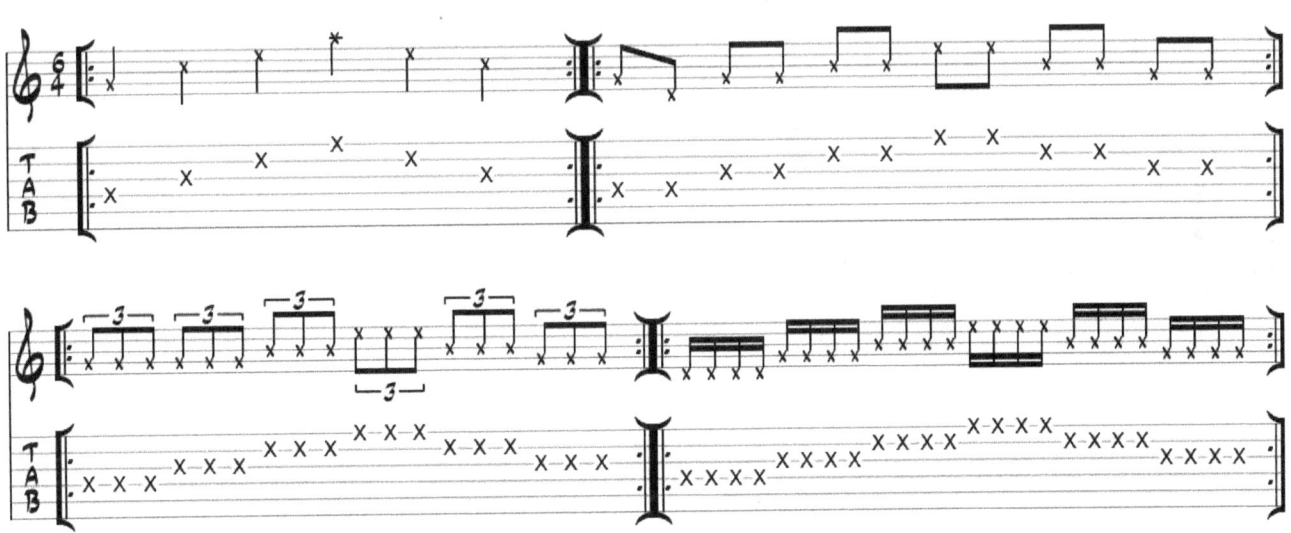

SHELL 1 4 (minor 3rd) eighth-notes

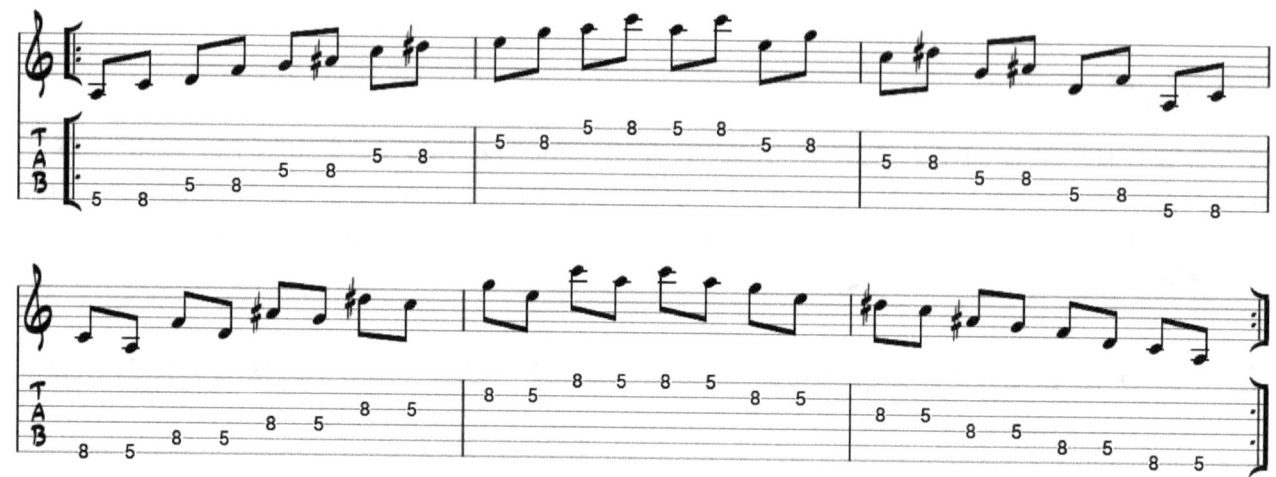

SHELL 1 4 Stretch (Major 3rd) eighth-notes

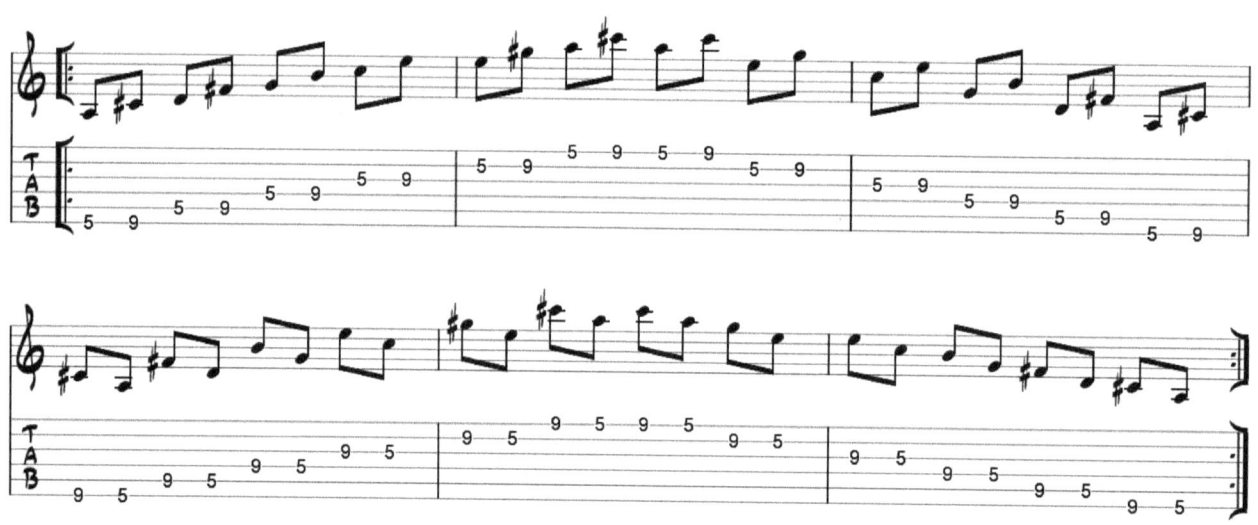

NATURAL NOTES ON FRETBOARD - 4 Strings

Here are the top 4 strings. So many or our arpeggios will live on these strings, so it is essential to know these notes. It is easier to start with the natural notes and adjust for sharps and flats later. Use the power of OCTAVE shapes.

Use the LONG Octave shape to connect notes of the HIGH E string to the G string and the B string to the D string.

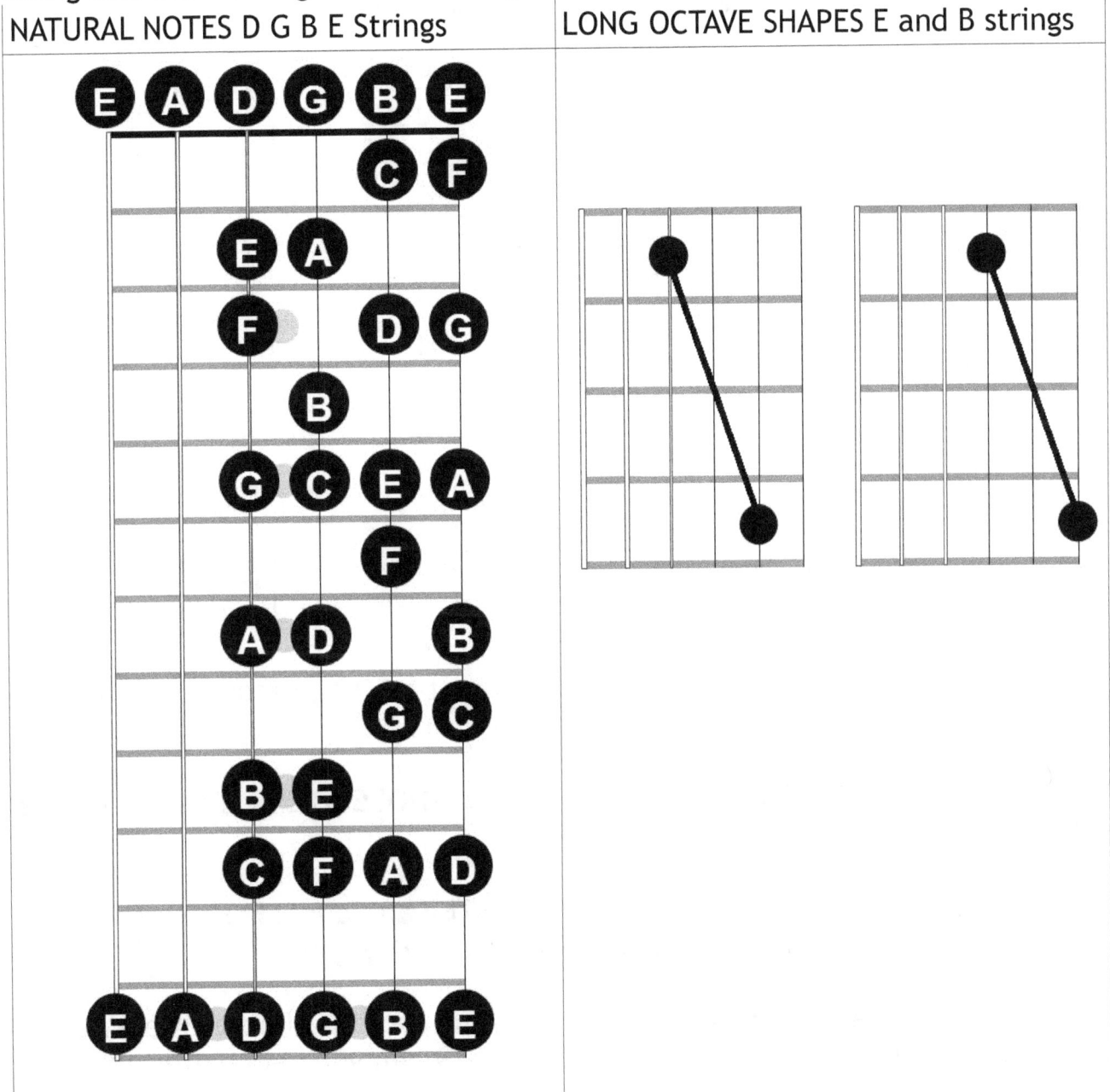

NATURAL NOTES D G B E Strings | LONG OCTAVE SHAPES E and B strings

EXERCISE

Go up and down EACH string playing AND saying each note aloud as you play it.
Play as Quarter-notes.

Melodic bass lines with 1 2 3 for each chord.

The first three notes from any ROOT will always be ROOT, second and THIRD of the chord.

For EVERYTHING **MAJOR** it will always be **TWO WHOLE-STEPS**. This will create ROOT, 2, 3.

For **MINOR**, it will *almost* always be **WHOLE-STEP and a HALF-STEP**. This will create R, 2, b3. (Half-step Whole-step R *b2 b3* for Phyrgian)

Even though the second of the scale is not in the chord it almost always sounds great as a passing tone and even a landing tone when you get comfortable.

REVIEW

THIRDS

The third in music is very special. It is the "toggle switch" between ANYTHING Major and minor in the music world. This is true for all chords and all scales. If there is no third of a chord/scale then it is neither Major nor minor (for example sus chords or power chords).

There are two types:

<u>Major third</u>:   2 whole-steps (4 frets from root on any 1 string)

<u>minor third</u>:   1 ½ steps (1 whole-step +1 half-step) (3 frets on any 1 string)

In the true sense the third is an interval (distance) between two notes/chords. We will see this interval (distance) between the 3rd and the 5th of a chord as well.

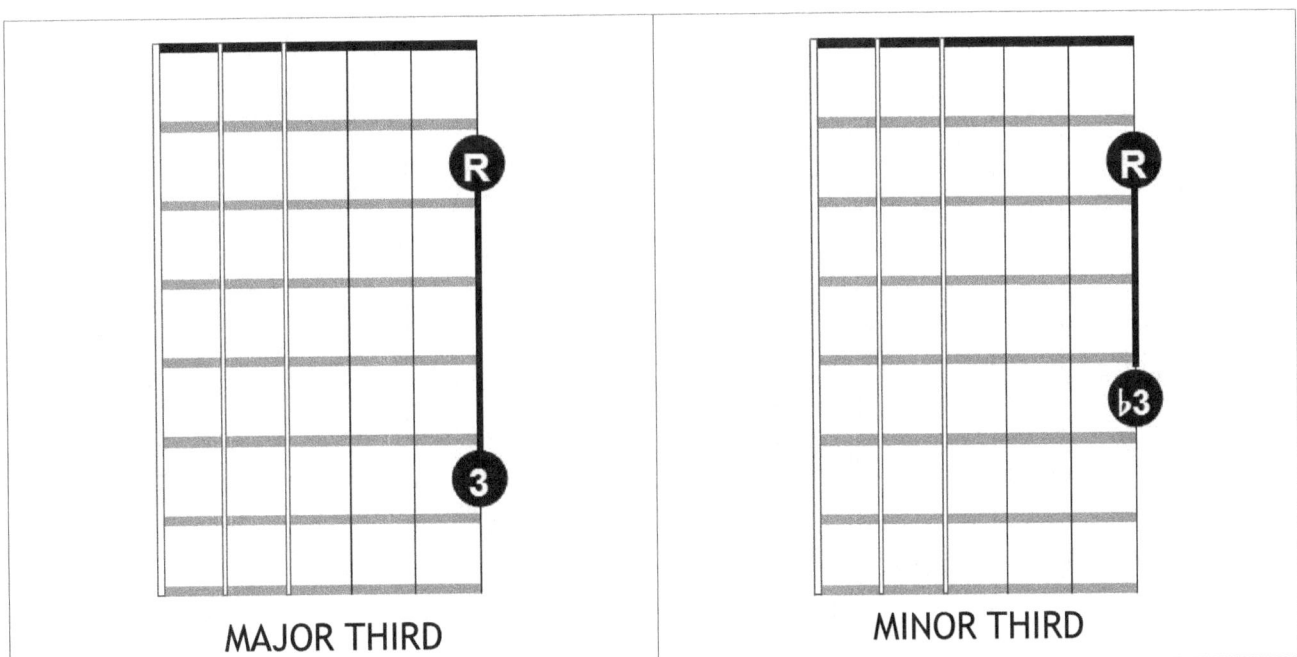

| MAJOR THIRD | MINOR THIRD |

FIFTHS

Any number in music refers to the where in line that note is in the scale. Our root is the first note and the 3rd is the third note away from the root. When we add the 5th we are adding a note a fifth away from the root. This creates the RULE OF THIRDS (building a chord by stacking every other note in a scale). When we have three notes (R 3 5) then we have a complete TRIAD.

You can see that each TRIAD is actually built with (2) THIRDS in a row. They FLIP FLOP depending on the quality of the chord. If a TRIAD is MAJOR, then it starts with a MAJOR THIRD followed by a MINOR THIRD to complete the TRIAD. The opposite is true for a minor chord. It starts with the MINOR third and is followed by a MAJOR third.

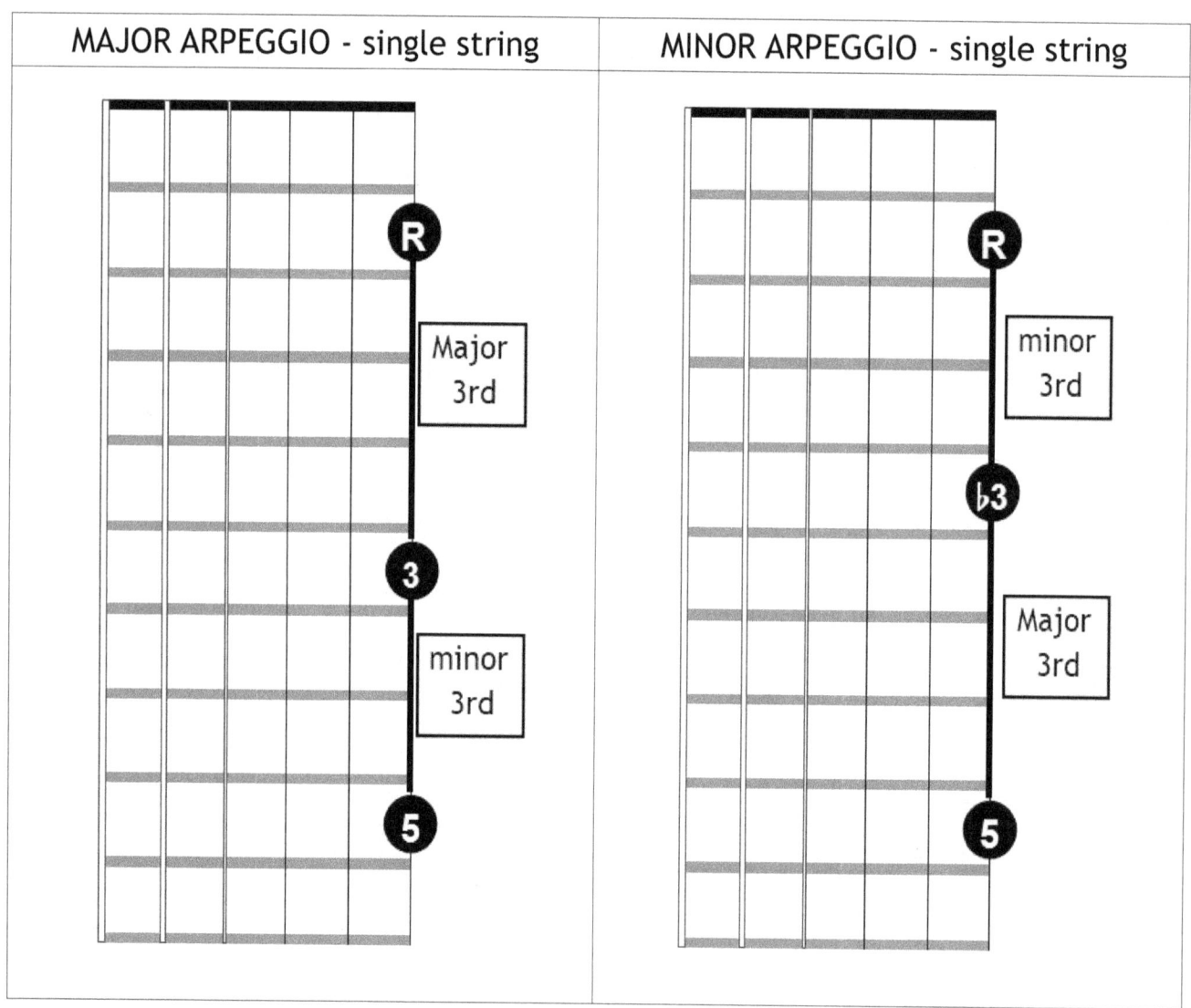

| MAJOR ARPEGGIO - single string | MINOR ARPEGGIO - single string |

PRACTICE

Root 3rd 5th (R 3 5) on one string for EACH CHORD (E and B strings)

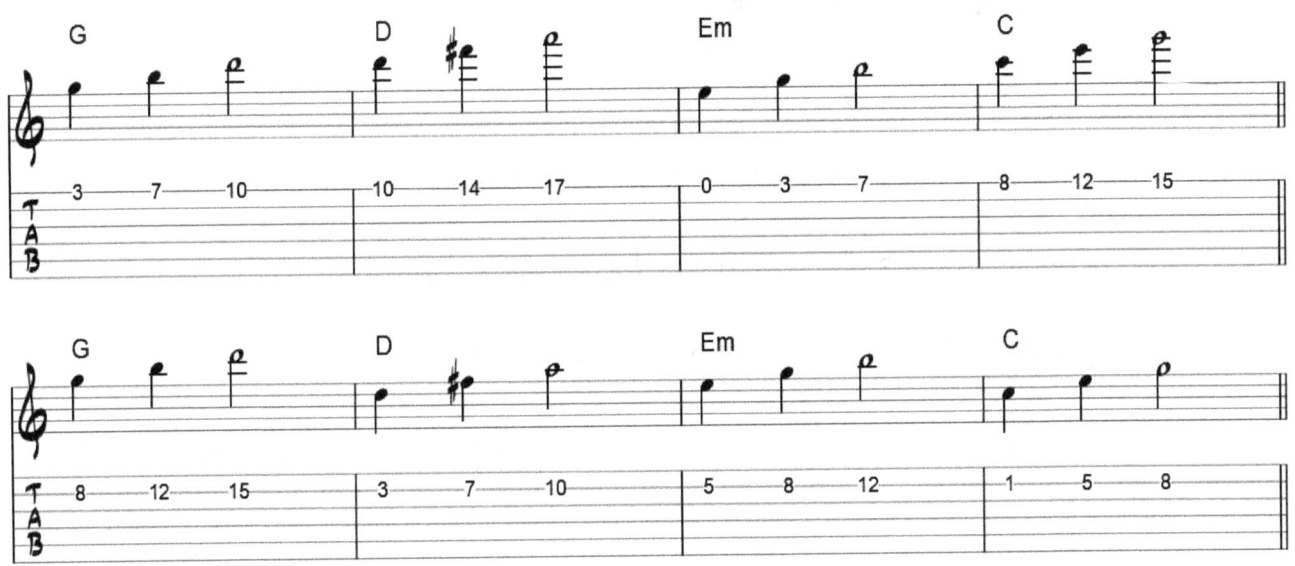

Root 3rd 5th (R 3 5) on one string for EACH CHORD (G and D strings)

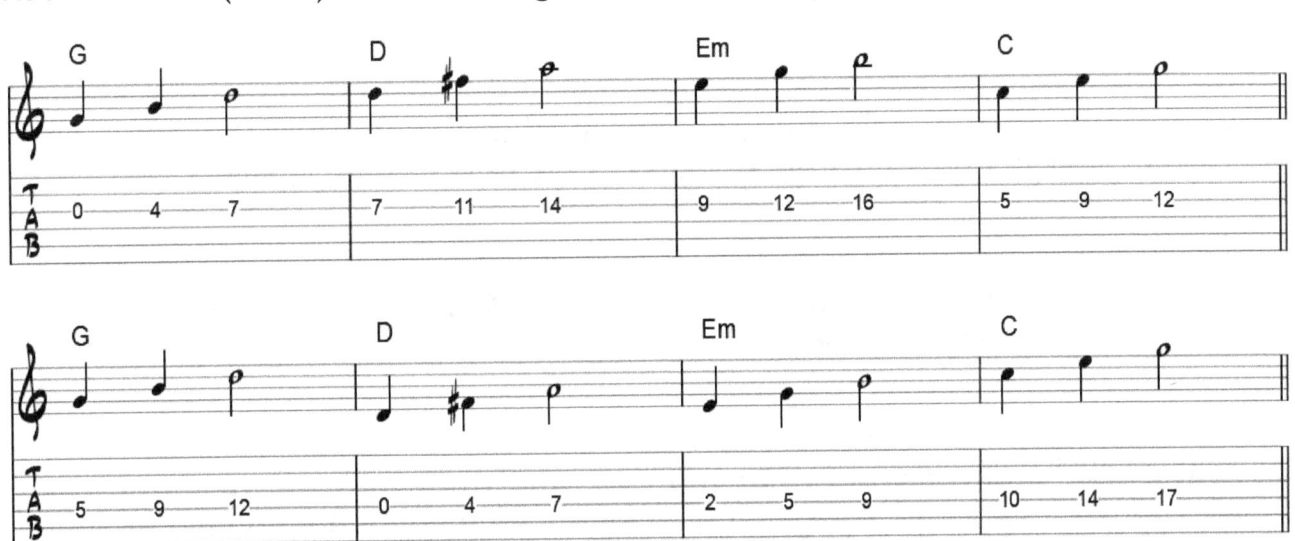

SUMMARY

We are musicians and we are guitar players.

Music is Melody, Harmony, and Rhythm.

We think like a musician first and then go to our instrument.

We must always know the chords in our heads as we play.

Learn to play the ROOT note on every chord change.

THIRDS are the "Toggle Switch" in music, dictating what is Major and what is minor.

The THIRD of a chord is always available on the same string the ROOT is. Even if you don't know the name of the THIRD, you can still get to it if you know the ROOT and the INTERVAL of the third.

Knowing the 1 2 3 of a scale is extremely valuable. It's three of the five notes of a Major pentatonic and three of seven notes of the Mode scales.

Adding the FIFTH of the chord completes the TRIAD. This give us the 3 notes that make up any MAJOR or MINOR chord.

It's really helpful and useful to see and play an arpeggio on one string. It's easy to see the spacing of the arpeggio on a single string while helping us expand our peripheral vision on the neck.

CHAPTER 3

TUNE IN

"I am a musician and a guitar player. Music is my language and my guitar is my voice. Music is Melody, Harmony and Rhythm. I develop my language skills and my instrument skills. They are two separate worlds working together to complete the circle of music."

Rhythm is the number one factor to sounding great as a musician.

WARM UP

Muted String Ladder (MSL) 6 Strings all 4 gears

ALL with *DOWN pick only,*
UP picks only, and
ALTERNATE pick

Do All 3 pickings before changing rhythm.

FIRST HALF

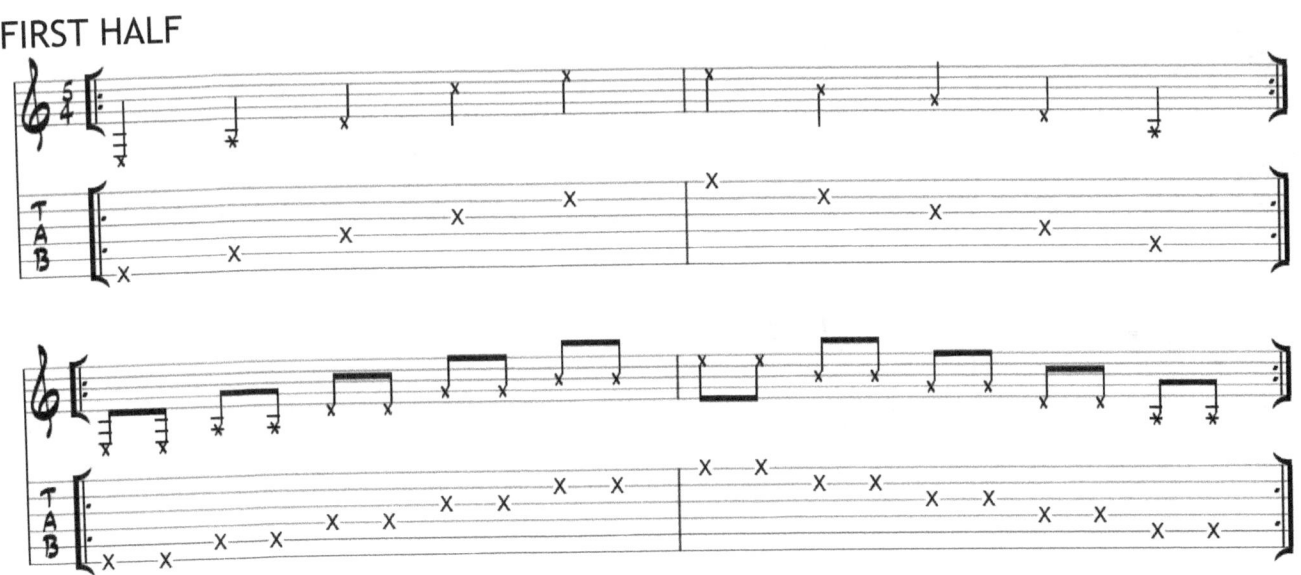

SECOND HALF (MSL)

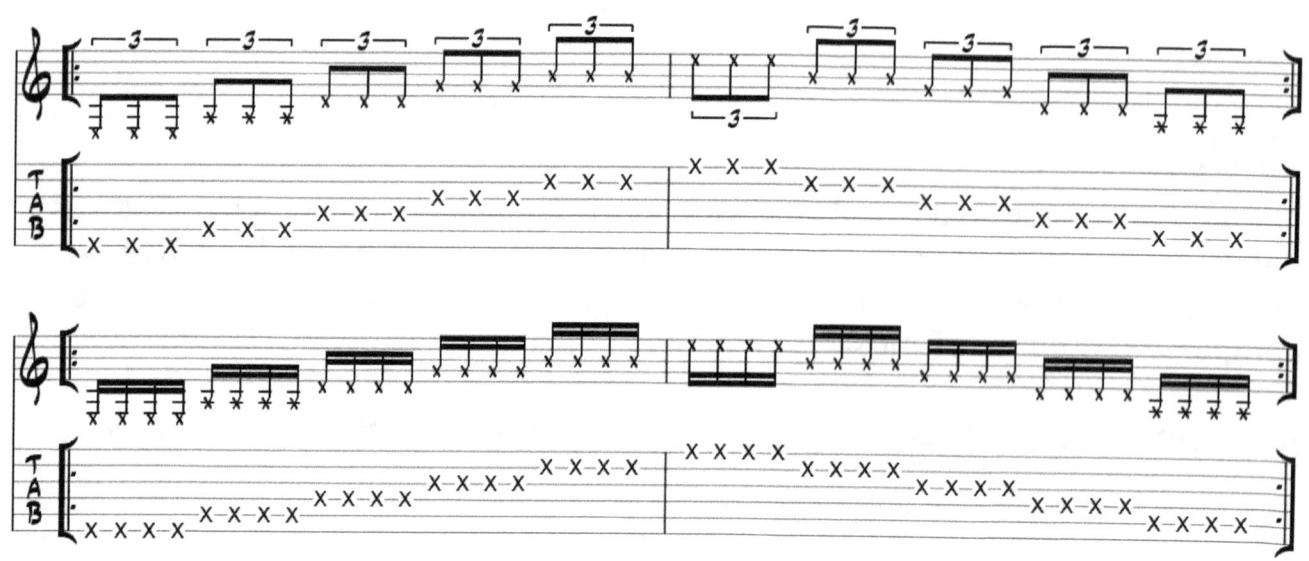

SHELL 1 Finger-at-a-time Quarter-notes (use a finger per fret)
Index finger for 5th fret (pointer finger)
Middle for 6th fret
Ring for 7th fret
Pinky for eighth fret

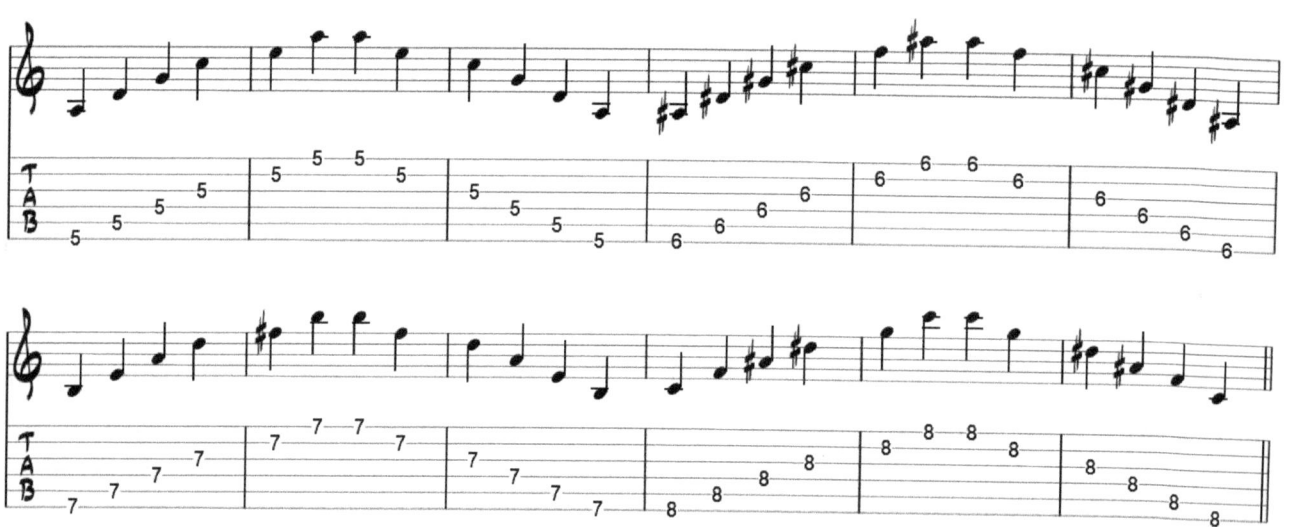

EXERCISE

1) Name the notes of chords C G D A E, and their minors.

C= C E G

G= G B D

D= D F# A

A= A C# E

E= E G# B

2) Play and Name all notes on any string up and down in quarter-notes.

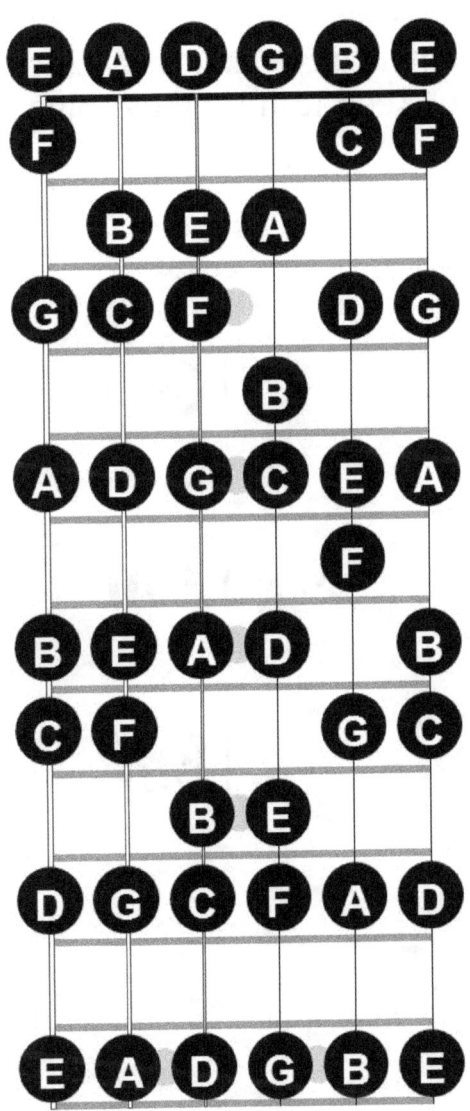

REVIEW

1. Play MELODIC BASSLINES using the ROOT. Play any rhythm as long as you start on the downbeat of each BAR.

2. Add the THIRDS to chords. Try playing as half-notes (2 beats per note).

3. Add the FIFTH to complete the TRIAD. Play each arpeggio on a single string. Play as quarter-notes.

4. Do the full TRIAD on any of the top 4 strings D G B E.

5. Self Generate by strumming first bar of each chord and then on second bar play the arpeggio. Keep it in time by using a metronome.

$\frac{4}{4}$|C |C |G |G |

|D |D |Am |Am |

|Em |Em |Bm |Bm   ‖

OCTAVES

A a guitar player it is essential to see how octaves live on the fretboard.

On the left there are the Neck Anatomy octaves, both SHORT and LONG. These are the keystone to unlocking your fretboard as a three octave instrument.

On the right are the "Behind" octaves. They skip two strings and go backwards (musically up in sound but the hand goes down the neck). These shapes are most helpful when in a pattern.

The Behind Octaves happen in your old school C chord and small bar F chord shapes, and even the open G chord.

These are all the same on any fret and especially true regarding the open strings.

Octaves are the pathway to seeing all of the notes on your fretboard.

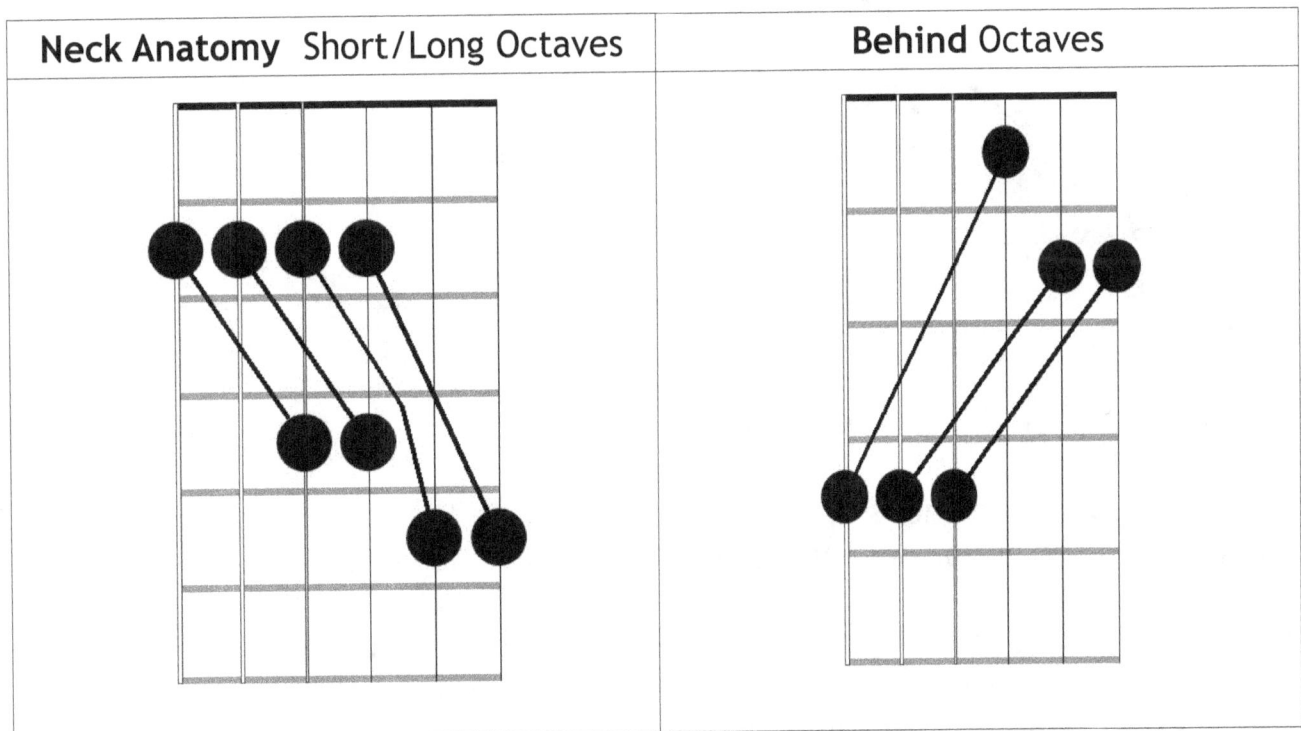

Neck Anatomy Short/Long Octaves	Behind Octaves

ABOVE ACROSS and BEHIND

Playing arpeggios all on one string has advantages and disadvantages. The advantage is you can easily see the intervals of the triad on one string. This can be used for nice bends, slides or even tapping.

The disadvantage is that you can't stay still. You have to keep moving to play a triad. Once you reassign one of the three notes onto an adjacent string it is playable in one position. You can see how you can pass one note at a time back to the previous string. It is a tremendous insight to the nature of the guitar.

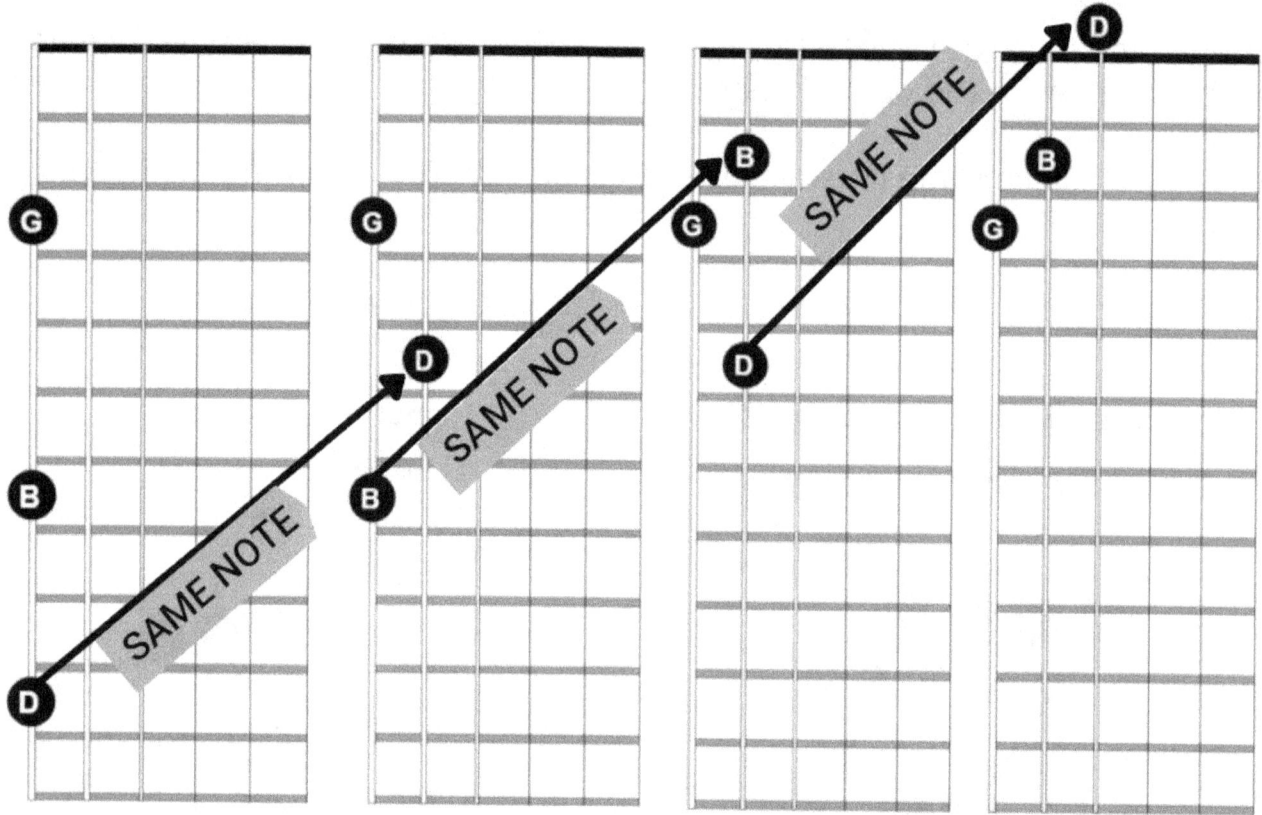

Above Across and Behind is a term I use to describe the three shapes of arpeggios on the guitar once you start reassigning the notes.

They are one octave and **can start from anywhere the root is**. Their names come from whether the THIRD and FIFTH are ABOVE the ROOT on the guitar, ACROSS from ROOT (some above, some behind) and from being BEHIND the ROOT.

ABOVE	ACROSS	BEHIND
Best for using the 1 2 3 on the same string. Sliding/bending the 2nd to the 3rd. Then adding the 5th.	Best for repeated arpeggio passages. Easy to play and quick especially with hammer-ons or pull-offs	Best for when you need all three notes on separate strings. Can act like a chord.

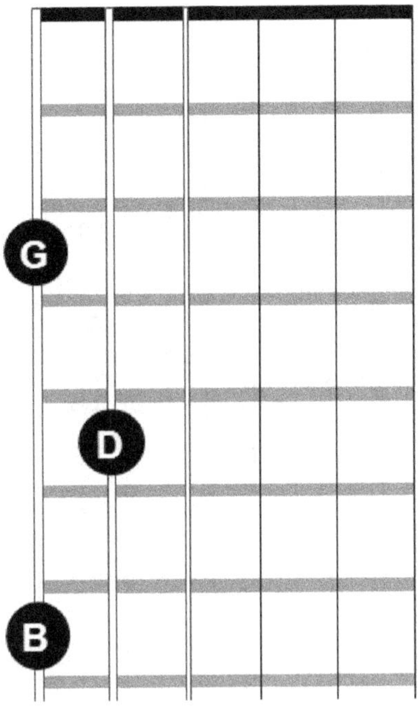

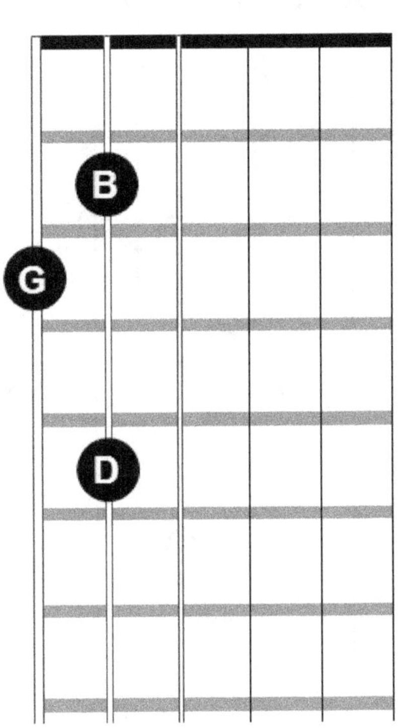

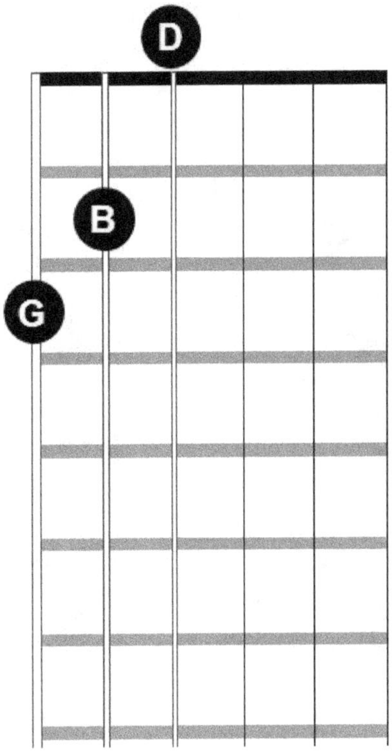

EXAMPLES:

ABOVE   ACROSS   BEHIND

ABOVE

Major and minor on all strings. *Note the triad shapes are the same on all strings except when the root starts on the G string.*

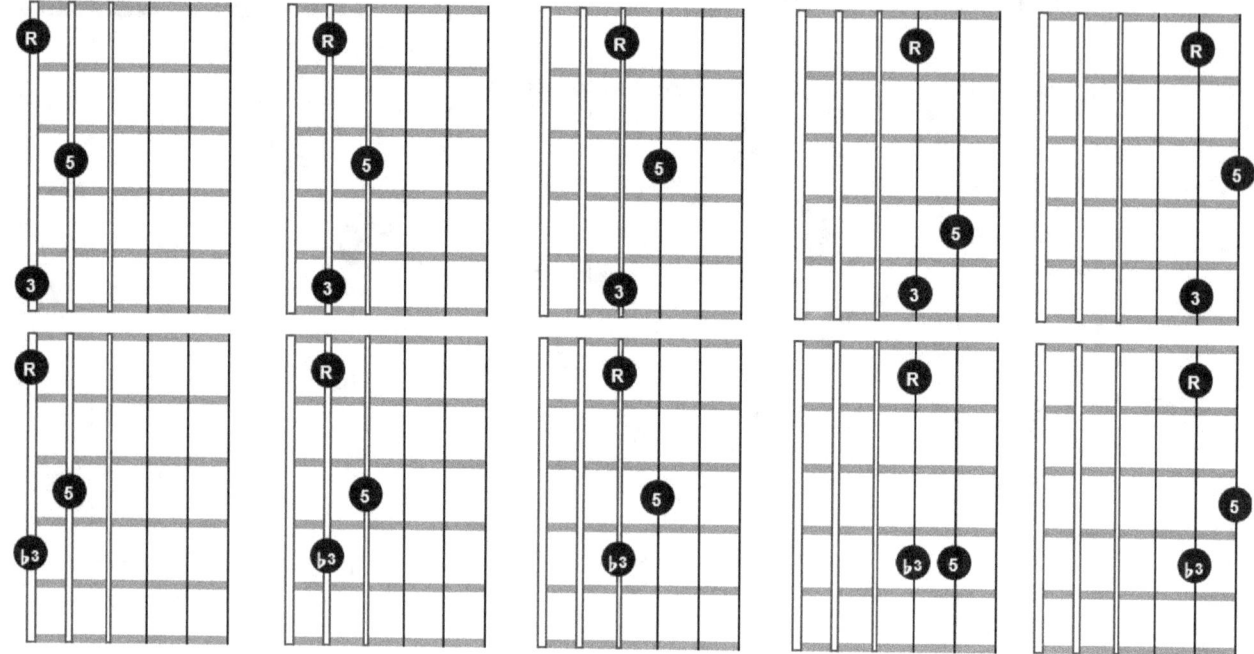

ACROSS

Major and minor on all strings. *Note the triad shapes are the same on all strings except when the root starts on the G string.*

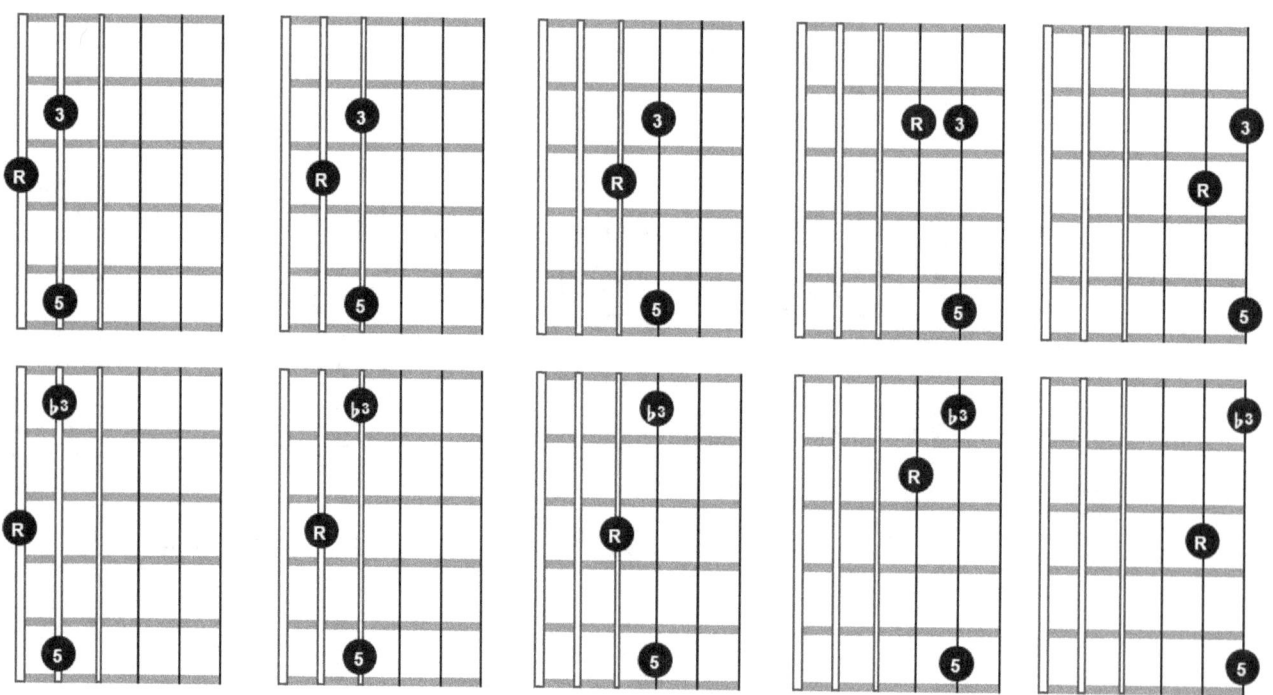

BEHIND

Major and minor on all strings. There are less shapes because they cover three strings instead of two.

Note how the triad shape changes when the root is on the D string and changes again when the root is on the G string.

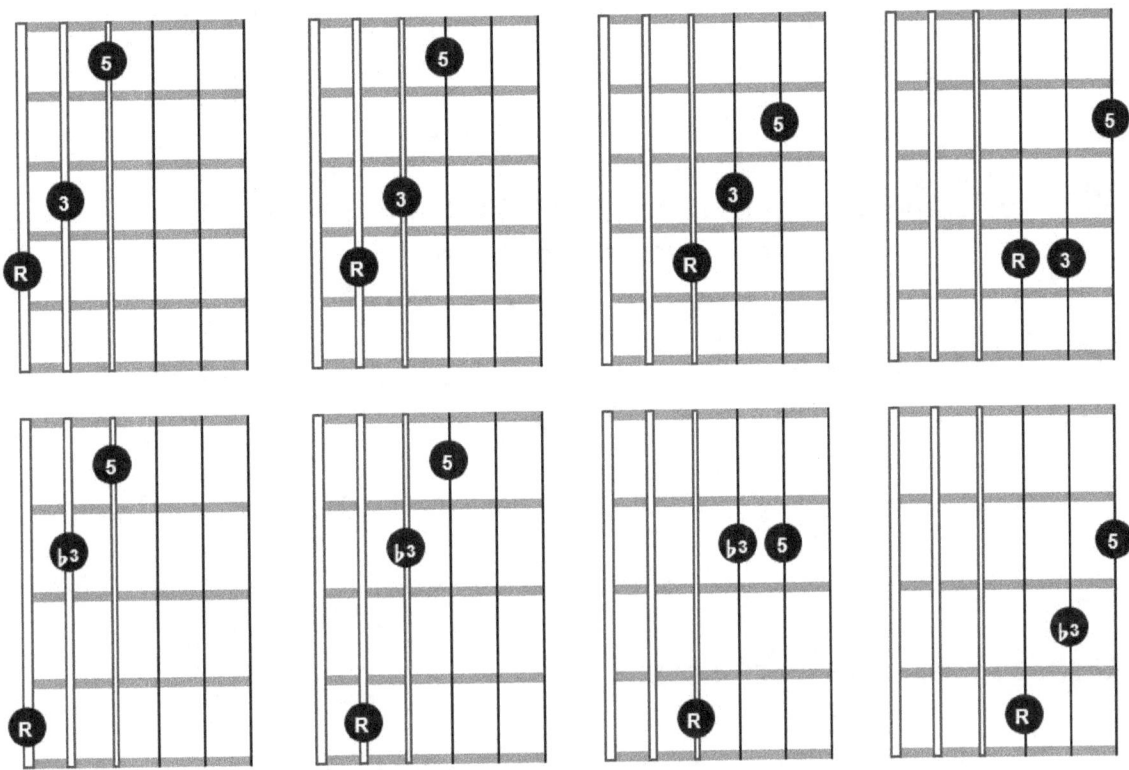

Any change of shape is due to the B string because it is tuned differently than the rest of the strings. Once a shape "touches" that string it changes. The note moves up a fret to compensate for being tuned a third instead of a fourth. (But if it starts on the B string it is OK.)

The guitar is tuned in FOURTHS **E** to **A** to **D** to **G** and **B** to **E** (EXCEPT G to B is a THIRD)

PRACTICE

ABOVE shape sliding into 3rd of each chord.

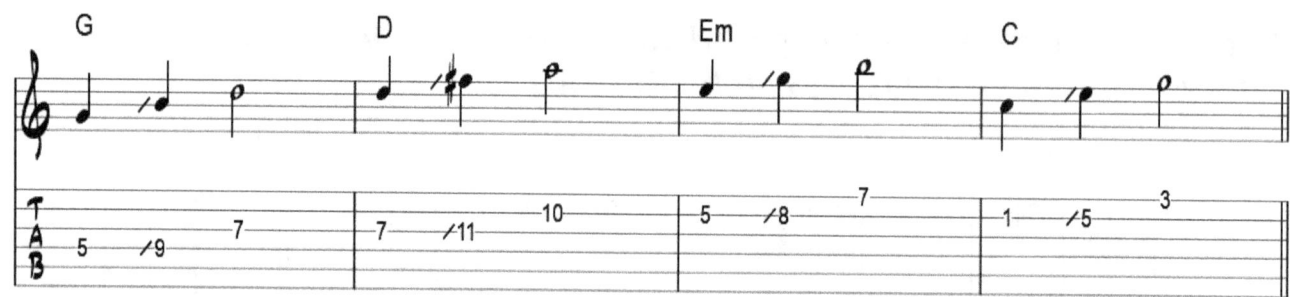

ACROSS shape using a repeated Tresillo (332). Note how each shape actually starts with the 5th of the chord and goes down to the root

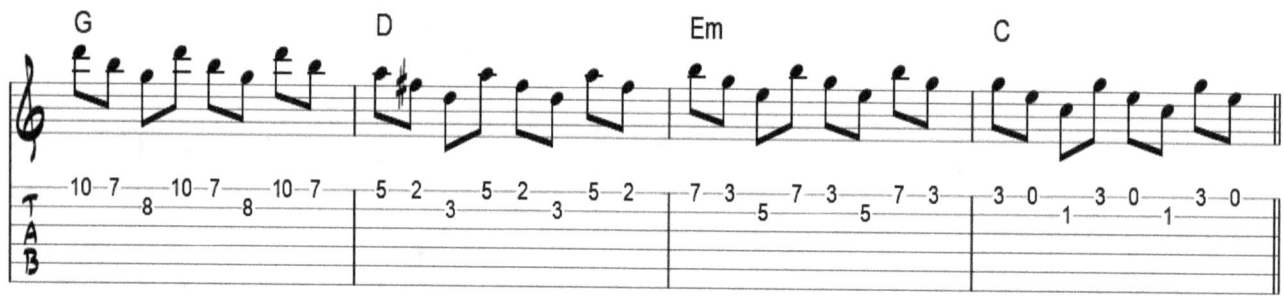

BEHIND shape sustaining each note.

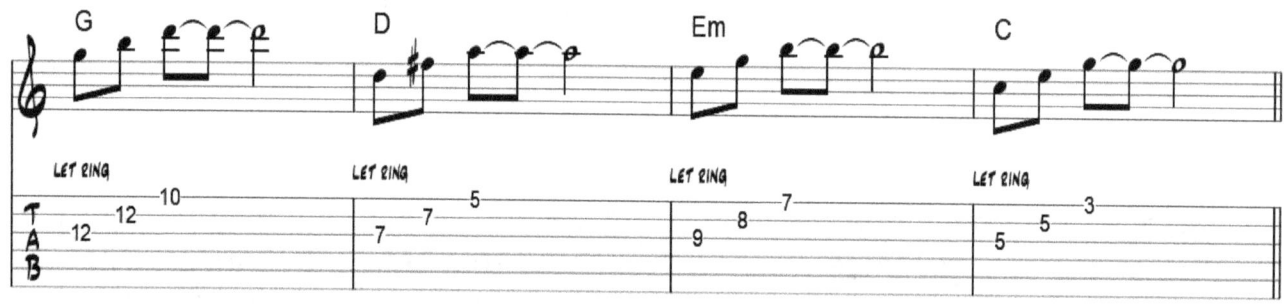

BACKING TRACKS

Follow-Along www.LeadGuitarWorkshop.com

Backing Track G Major

$\frac{4}{4}$|G |D |Em |C   ‖

Backing Track E minor

$\frac{4}{4}$|Em |D |Am |C   ‖

Backing Track A Major

$\frac{4}{4}$|A |E |F#m |D   ‖

Backing Track C Major

$\frac{4}{4}$|C |C |F$_{MA}^7$ |F$_{MA}^7$ |

|C |C |F$_{MA}^7$ |F$_{MA}^7$ |

|Am |G |F |Dm |

|Am |G |F |G   ‖

SUMMARY

We are musicians and we are guitar players.

Music is Melody, Harmony, and Rhythm.

We think like a musician first and then go to our instrument.

We must always know the chords in our heads as we play.

Learn to play the ROOT note on every chord change.

THIRDS are the "Toggle Switch" in music, dictating what is Major and what is minor.

The THIRD of a chord is always available on the same string as the ROOT. Even if you don't know the name of the THIRD, you can still get to it if you know the ROOT and the INTERVAL of the third.

Adding the FIFTH of the chord completes the TRIAD. This give us the 3 notes that make up any MAJOR or MINOR chord.

Knowing the octave shapes on guitar is crucial to understanding your fretboard.

Above, Across and Behind is one of the cleanest ways to look at arpeggios on the guitar neck.

There are only 12 Major chords, and since we know the "toggle switch" we know the 12 minor chords too.

CHAPTER 4

TUNE IN

"I am a musician and a guitar player. Music is my language and my guitar is my voice. Music is Melody, Harmony and Rhythm. I develop my language skills and my instrument skills. They are two separate worlds working together to complete the circle of music."

Rhythm is the number one factor to sounding great as a musician.

WARM UP + EXERCISE

Muted String Ladder (MSL) 6 strings LEAPFROG Quarter-notes and Eighth-notes

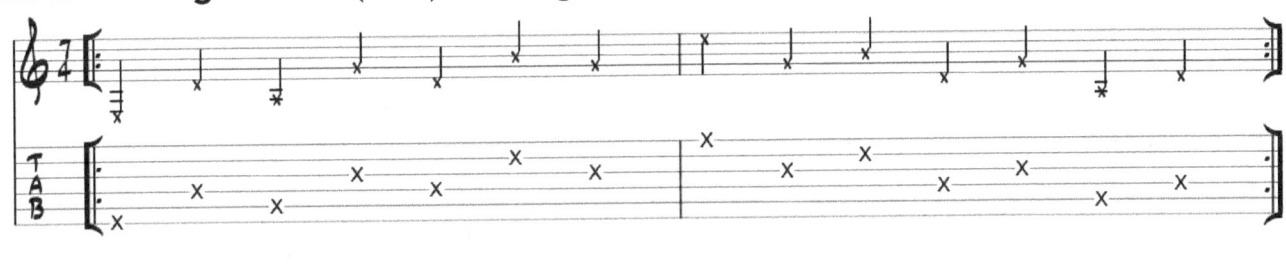

Alternate pick vs Economy pick

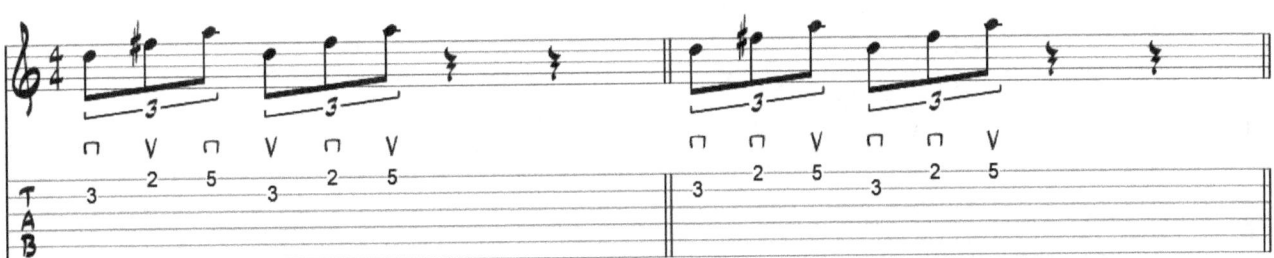

Alternate picking arpeggios repeatedly creates a flip flop in picking.
Economy picking reduces excess picking by grouping same directions in picking.

SHELL ARPEGGIOS

Use the SHELL method to practice your arpeggios. It's the same process but using an arpeggios shape.

- FINGERING: Pick a Shape (for example ACROSS MAJOR)
- PERFORMANCE: In position and up and down 1 string(s)
- RHYTHM: first one is quarter-notes and second is triplets

SHELL Across Shape Major   UP and DOWN strings   Quarter-notes with rest (1/2)

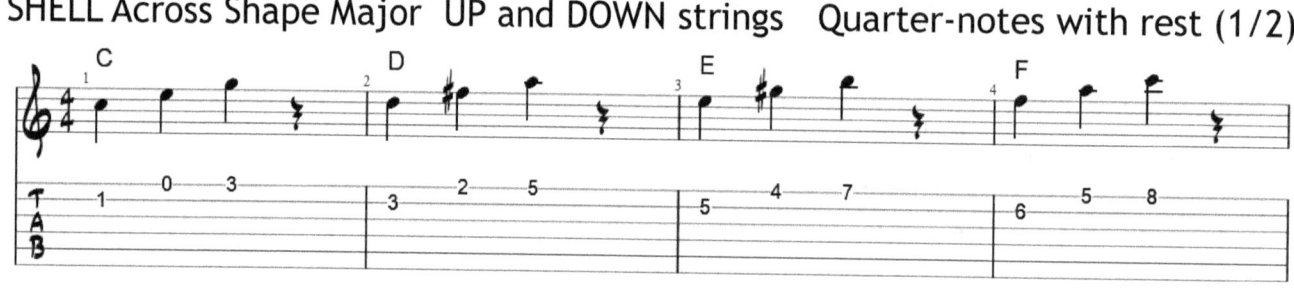

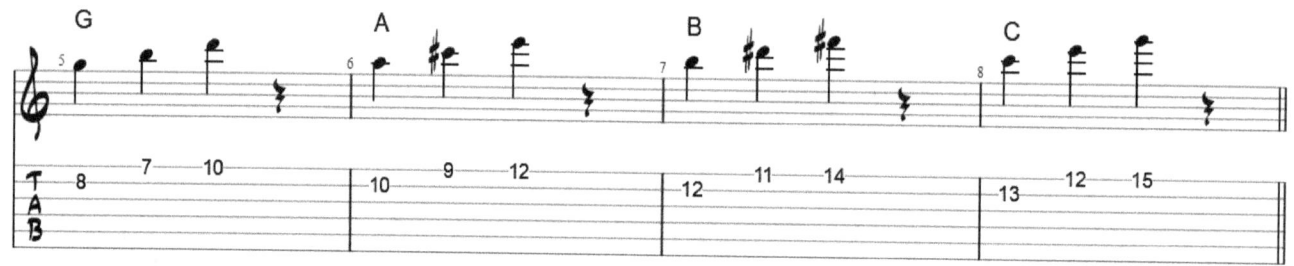

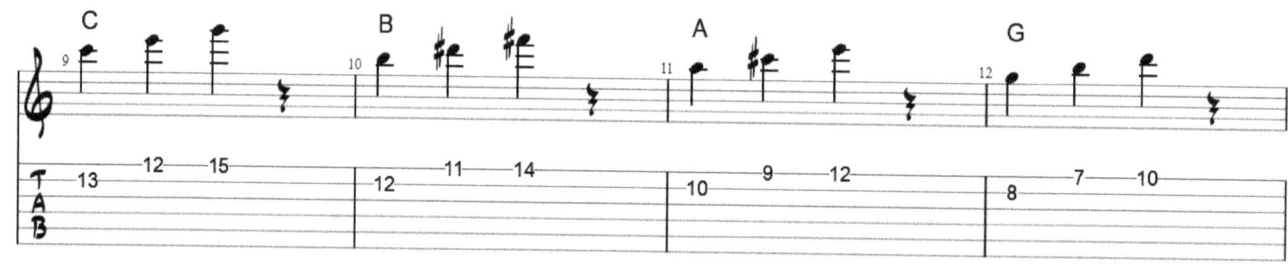

SHELL Across Shape Major   UP and DOWN strings   Quarter-notes with rest (2/2)

Remember, the SHELL method is meant to help guitar players move around the fretboard unhindered by hand habits. This SHELL ARPEGGIO version allows the arpeggio itself to be played ascending and descending. The entire shape is able to move independently around the fretboard. This results in all of the musical ways you can move the arpeggio around the neck.

SHELL ARPEGGIOS - In Position

Use the Across shape and move a Major triad across each string staying on the same fret (except G to B strings), resulting in a movement of 4ths. Each arpeggio can ascend or descend their own three notes and their entire triad can move independently.

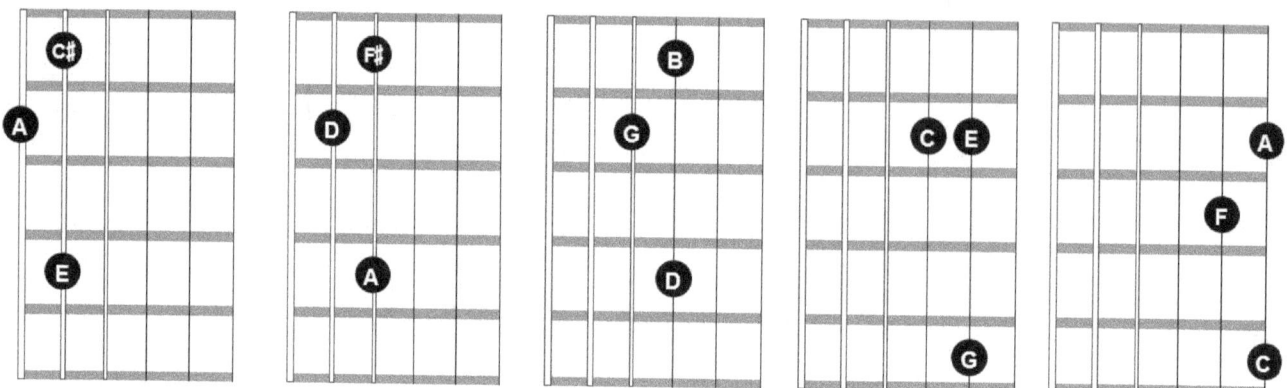

Ascending arpeggios in both directions

Descending arpeggios in both directions

COOL TIP: Moving across the fretboard like this is moving in the cycle of 4ths. The last chord in this cycle if F Major. If you restart this whole pattern again on the 6th fret instead of the 5th you will start on Bb. This is the next in the cycle of 4ths (Bb Eb Ab Db Gb). It will continue across as you restart again, one fret higher on the 7th fret. This is the last cycle to access the B and E to finally get back to A an octave higher (all 12 Major arpeggios).

ABOVE ACROSS BEHIND REVIEW

Once you see that any arpeggio can happen in one of three ways starting on a note you will start to look at scale patterns in a new way. If we look at PATTERN #1 of the MODES in the KEY of G, we get:

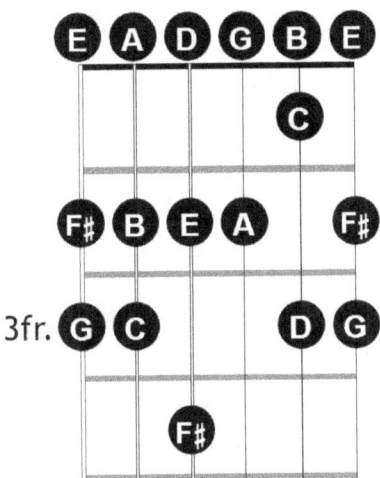

If we remind ourselves of the chords in the key of G by using WWHWWWH and the Diatonic Formula I ii iii IV V vi vii(dim) then we get.

G Am Bm C D Em F#dim

If we start Pattern #1 on the lowest note (E) we can build an E minor triad using an ABOVE shape. The F# diminished (F# A C) will be an ACROSS and the G Major chord will be a BEHIND. Starting on the 5th string with be an A minor in the ABOVE shape. You follow this process through the entire pattern.

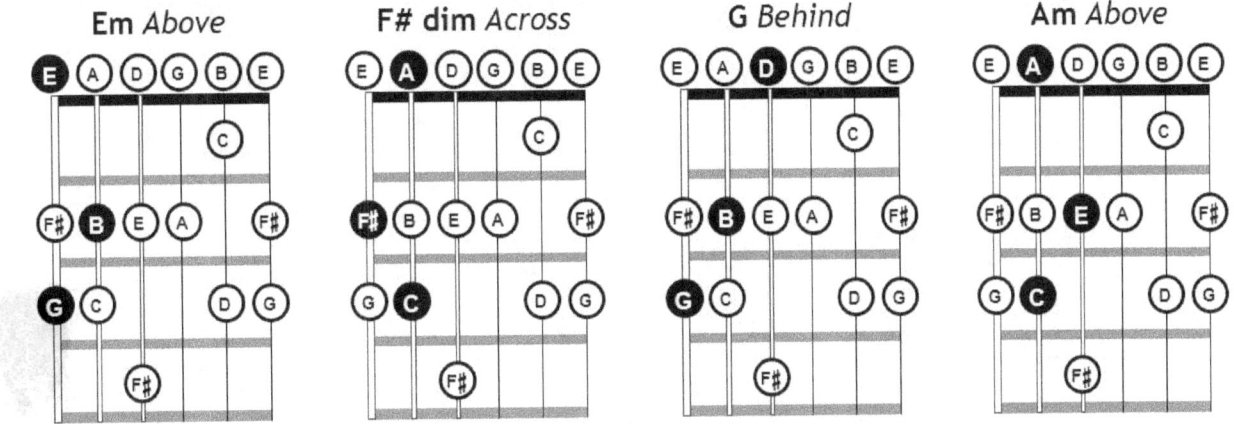

DIATONIC ARPEGGIOS PATTERN #1 - Key G

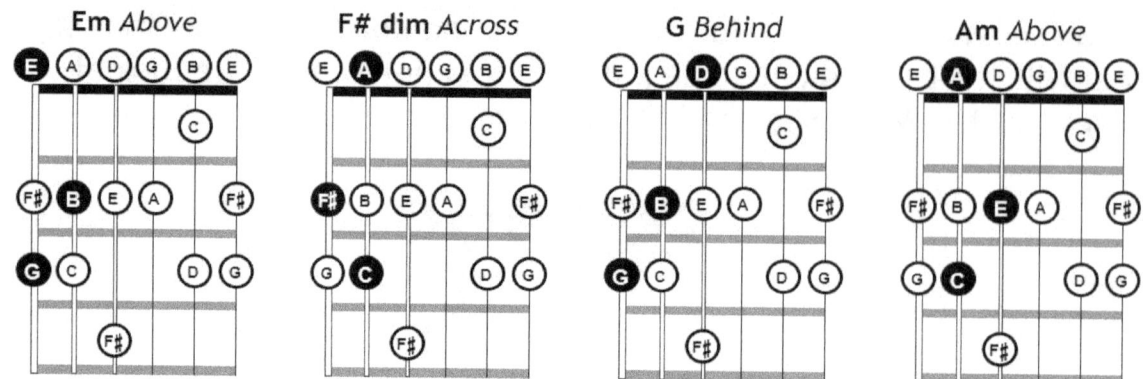

Em *Above*   F# dim *Across*   G *Behind*   Am *Above*

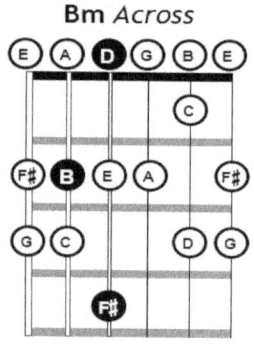 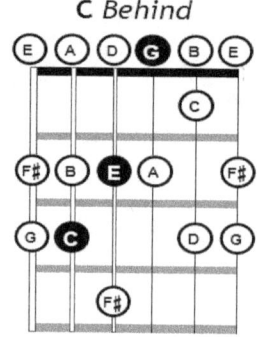 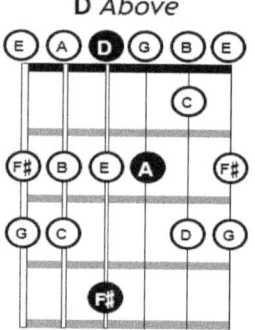

Bm *Across*   C *Behind*   D *Above*

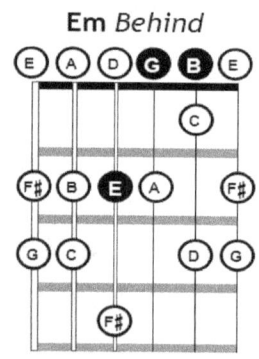 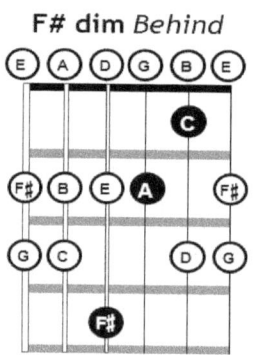 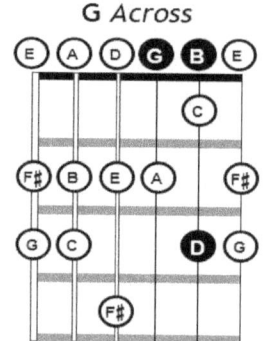

Em *Behind*   F# dim *Behind*   G *Across*

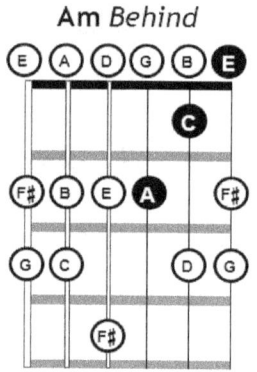 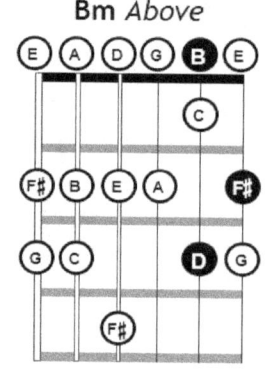 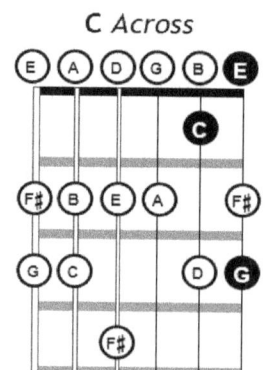

Am *Behind*   Bm *Above*   C *Across*

GUIDE TONES

Another way to use arpeggios is with guide tones. Guide tones are the notes of a chord used as landing spots to help establish the sounds of the chords throughout your solo. Think of them like "fence posts." They help frame out a solid melodic line through the chord changes and you can embellish them and surround them in different ways.

Guide tones need you to be musical, and to know the name of the notes in each chord. You need to be a good guitar player and not only be able to locate the notes of each arpeggio but string together a cohesive musical line as well.

Guide Tones bridge the scale sound of solos and the arpeggio sound of solos. They help you play the changes and outline chords while retaining a familiar feel of scale based playing.

Here is an example of a Guide Tone Line and an example of embellishment. Each guide tone is a chord tone and it only moves to another chord tone on the downbeat of the change. Ideally it will move either by half-steps or whole-steps. You can keep common tones or focus of different tones.

GUIDE TONE LINE:

G chord = **G** *(root)*   D chord = **A** *(5th)*   Em chord = **B** *(5th)*   C chord = **C** *(root)*

GUIDE TONE PRACTICE

G Major Backing Track Guide Tone Line example

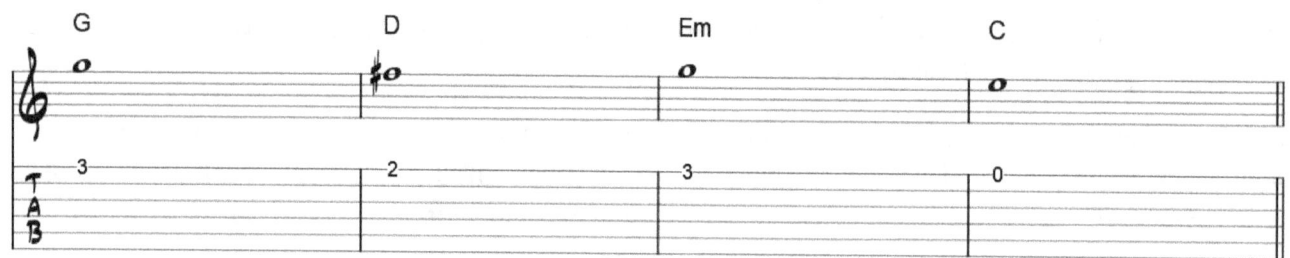

E minor Backing Track Guide Tone Line example

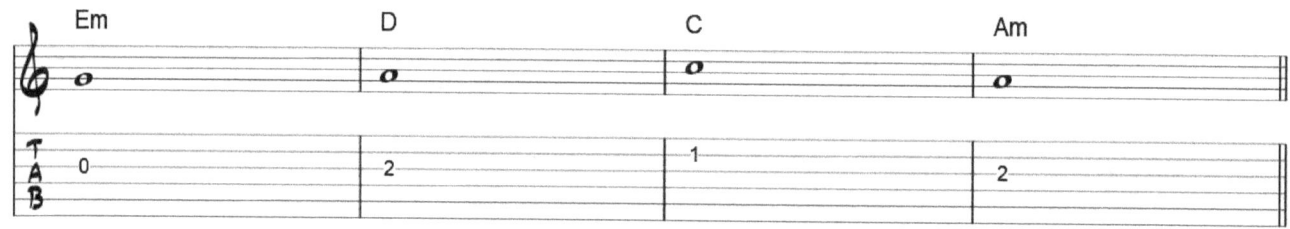

A Major Backing Track Guide Tone Line example

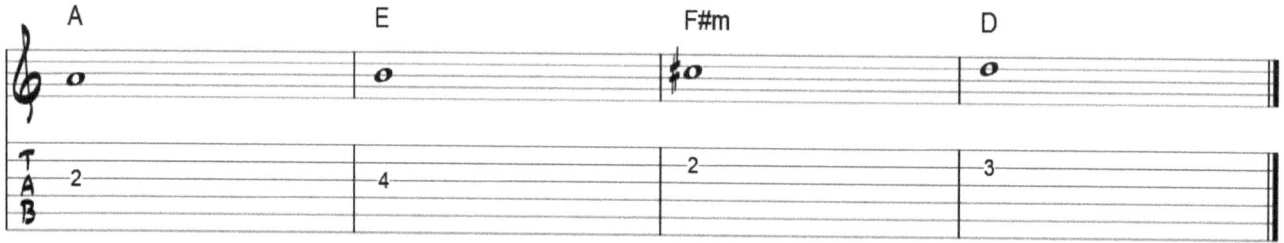

C Major Backing Track Guide Tone Line example

Follow-Along Backing Track
www.LeadGuitarWorkshop.com

SUMMARY

We are musicians and we are guitar players.

Music is Melody, Harmony, and Rhythm.

We think like a musician first and then go to our instrument.

We must always know the chords in our heads as we play.

Learn to play the ROOT note on every chord change, eventually the THIRD and FIFTH.

THIRDS are the "Toggle Switch" in music, the ONLY thing dictating what is **Major** and what is **minor**.

The THIRD of a chord is always available on the same string as the ROOT. Even if you don't know the name of the THIRD, you can still get to it if you know the ROOT and the INTERVAL of the third.

Adding the FIFTH of the chord completes the TRIAD. This give us the 3 notes that make up any MAJOR or MINOR chord.

Knowing the octave shapes on guitar is crucial to understanding your fretboard.

Above, Across and Behind is one of the cleanest ways to look at arpeggios on the guitar neck, especially when you see them in any of your MODE patterns.

GUIDE TONES are one of the secrets of sounding great. They bridge the typical scale solo sound with the arpeggio sound allowing you to "play the changes."

There are only 12 Major chords, and since we know the "toggle switch" we know the 12 minor chords too.

CHAPTER 5

TUNE IN

"I am a musician and a guitar player. Music is my language and my guitar is my voice. Music is Melody, Harmony and Rhythm. I develop my language skills and my instrument skills. They are two separate worlds working together to complete the circle of music."

Rhythm is the number one factor to sounding great as a musician.

WARM UP

Muted String Ladder (MSL)

MSL 6 strings LEAPFROG all 4 gears

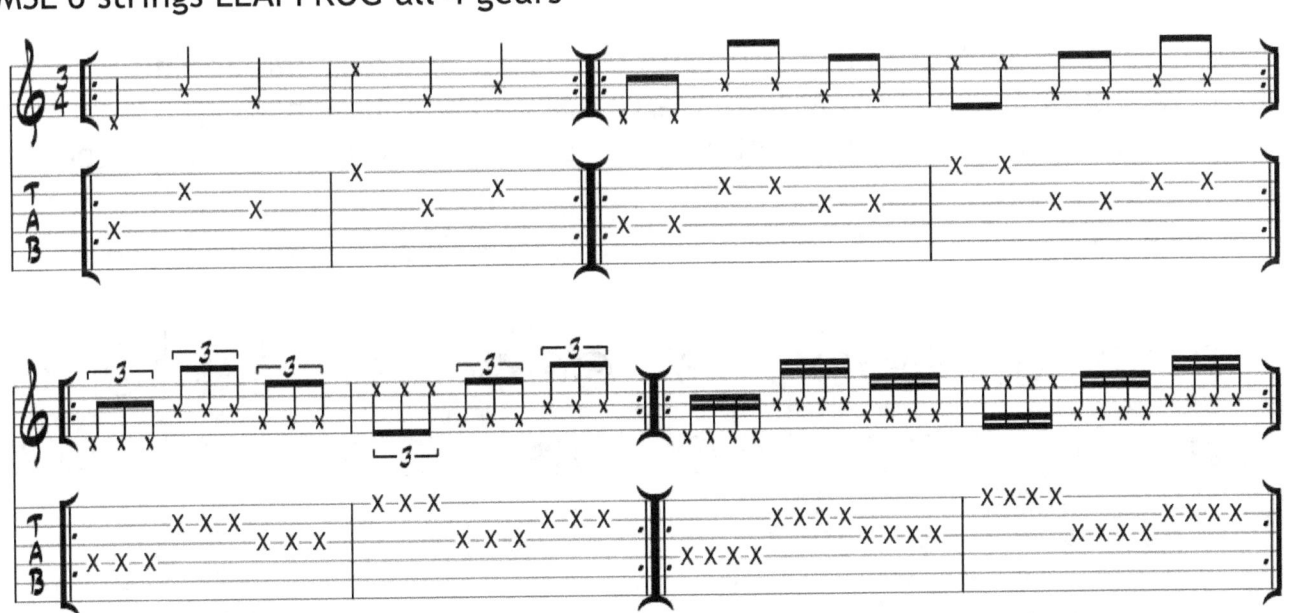

SHELL

Shell 1 finger as eighth-notes

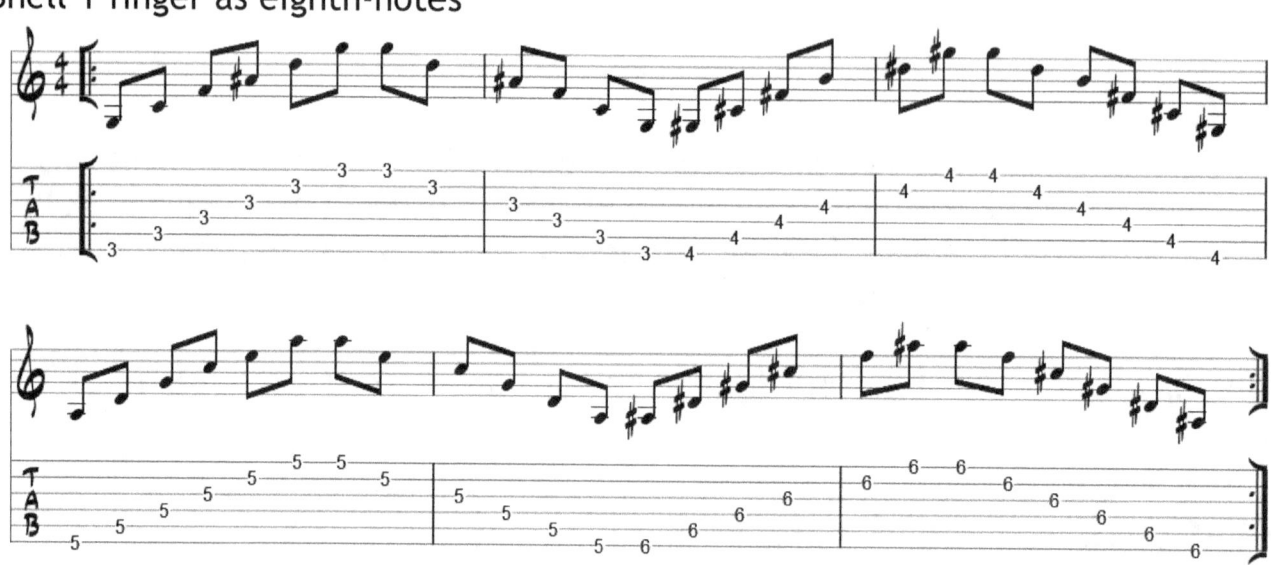

EXERCISE

Pattern #2 G Major Arpeggios in position using Above Across and Behind
Here are the first four. Complete patterns are on the following page.
Play each one as quarter-notes followed by quarter-note rest, one chord per
bar.

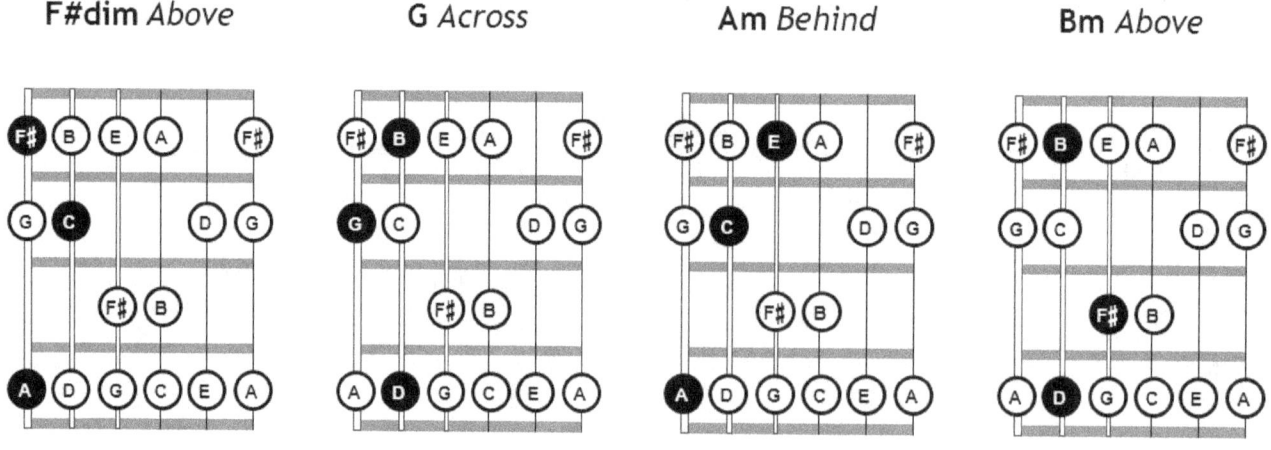

F#dim _Above_   G _Across_   Am _Behind_   Bm _Above_

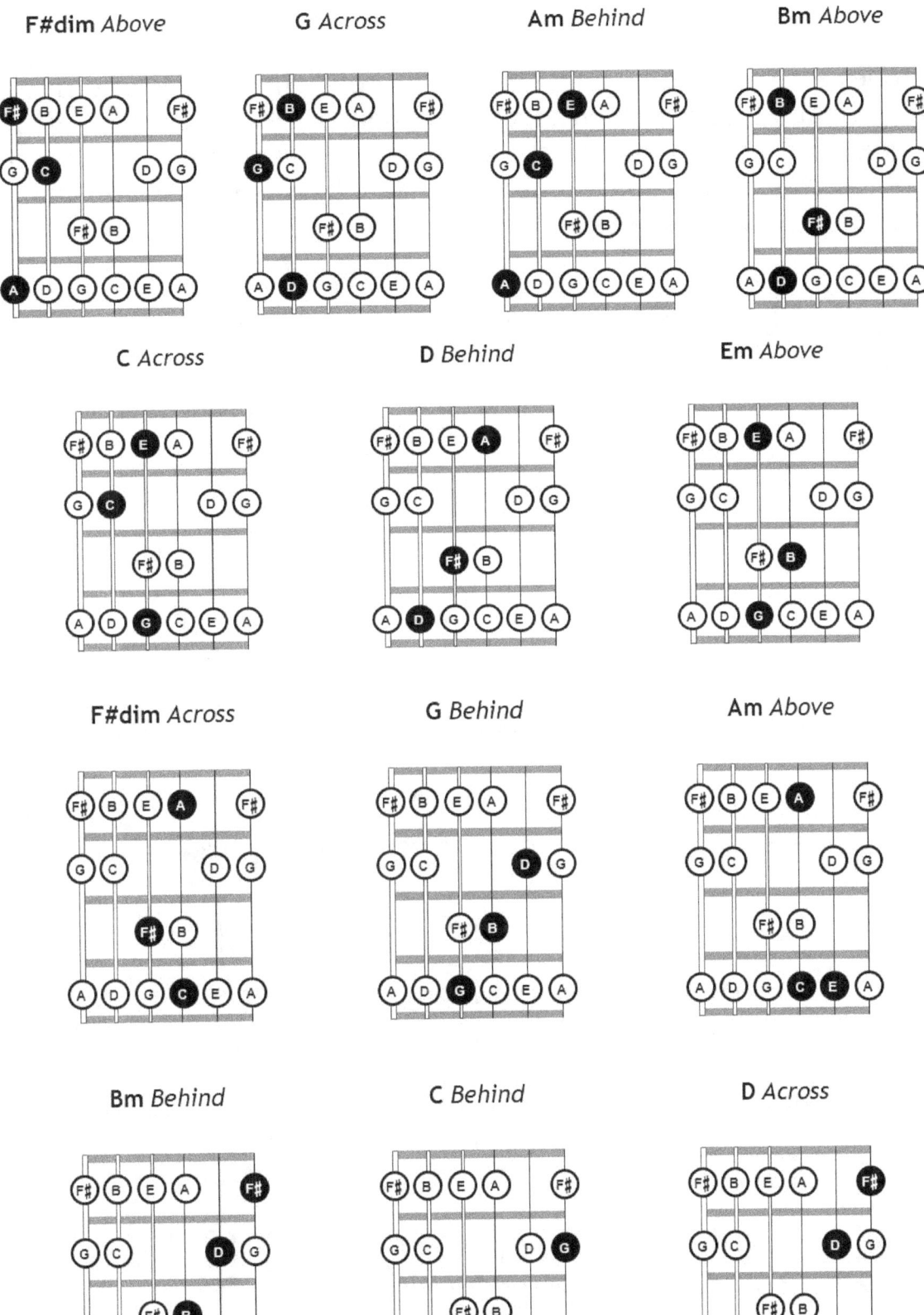

GUIDE TONE REVIEW

Guide tones are the melodic lines that help thread chord progressions together. Guide tones are chord tones that connect by whole-step of half-step (can be more). They match each chord as they go by and help establish the sound of the chords. The guide tones act as fence posts to help you build more involved ideas around a stable and simple line.

Example: Guide tone line and solo #1 (E minor backing track)

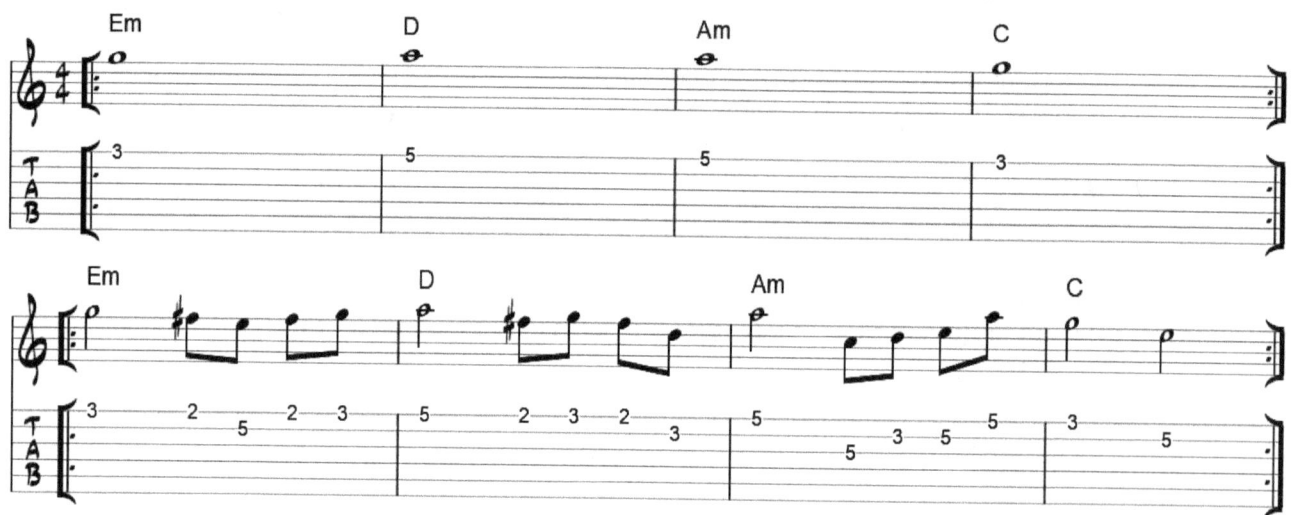

Example: Guide tone line and solo #2 (E minor backing track)

CHORD INVERSIONS part 1

Chord inversions take the notes of a chord and rotate their order of low to high sounds. There are three inversions of a triad: Root position, first inversion and second inversion.

Root position	1st Inversion	2nd Inversion
5	R	3
3	5	R
R	3	5

If we look at a G Major triad we get

Root position	1st Inversion	2nd Inversion
D	G	B
B	D	G
G	B	D
G	G/B	G/D

Chord inversions help us equally as a rhythm guitar player and as lead player.

As a rhythm player, these smaller chords (only 3 notes compared to a full bar) allow the sound of the chords to move up and down within the chord. They allow different notes to be in the melody for chord melody playing. They are great for 2nd or 3rd guitar players in a band because they offer chord options where players can find their space in the mix.

As lead players we can use these to help build guide tone lines as well as just seeing all of the chord tones on top of the chords and scale patterns. People like David Gilmour will often play a basic pentatonic scale but add these inversions and trace them during his solos ("Comfortably Numb" first solo/melody) to match the chords.

CHORD INVERSIONS

To find our inversion shapes we first need to know these three forms of bar chords. The E and A are common to most players but the C is new. It can be tricky at first but is a fantastic chord voicing to add to your sound. It blew me away when I realized the C and D chords share the same shape.

- Pick a Chord and find its ROOT on the E string and the A string.
- The E string ROOT gets the E form Bar chord.
- The A string ROOT gets **BOTH** the C form and the A form.
- Once the three chords are located isolate the TOP 3 strings and you have the inversions for the chord.

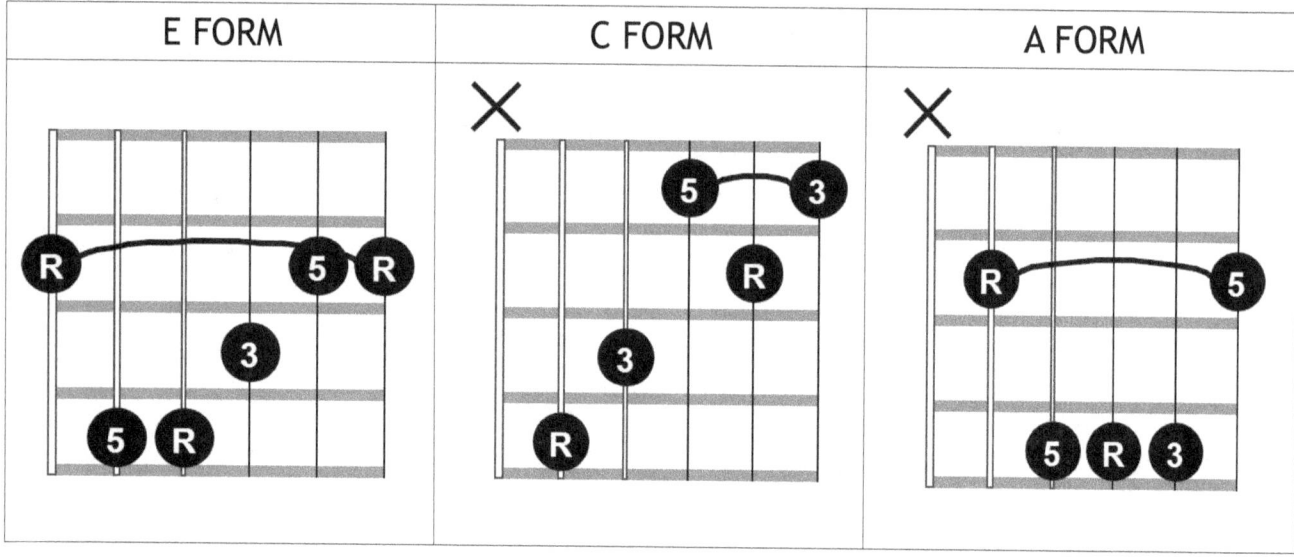

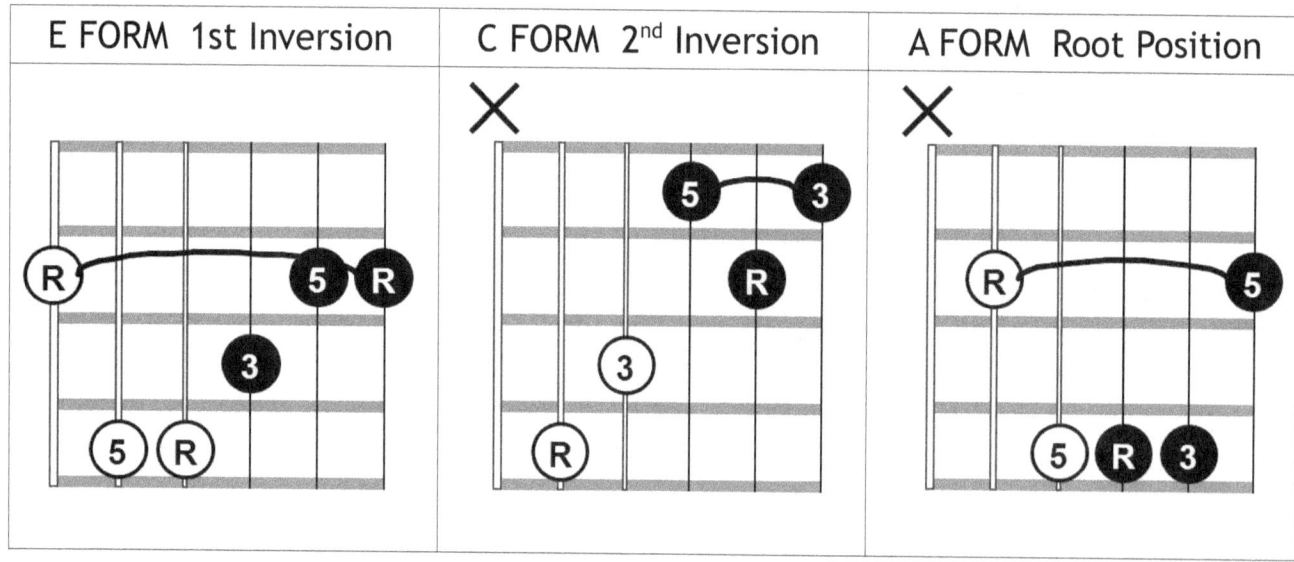

Here is a G Major chord and G minor chord.

ROOT on the E and A string is highlighted by a SQUARE.

The C form and A form share the ROOT of the fifth string.

To make a chord minor, lower the 3rd.

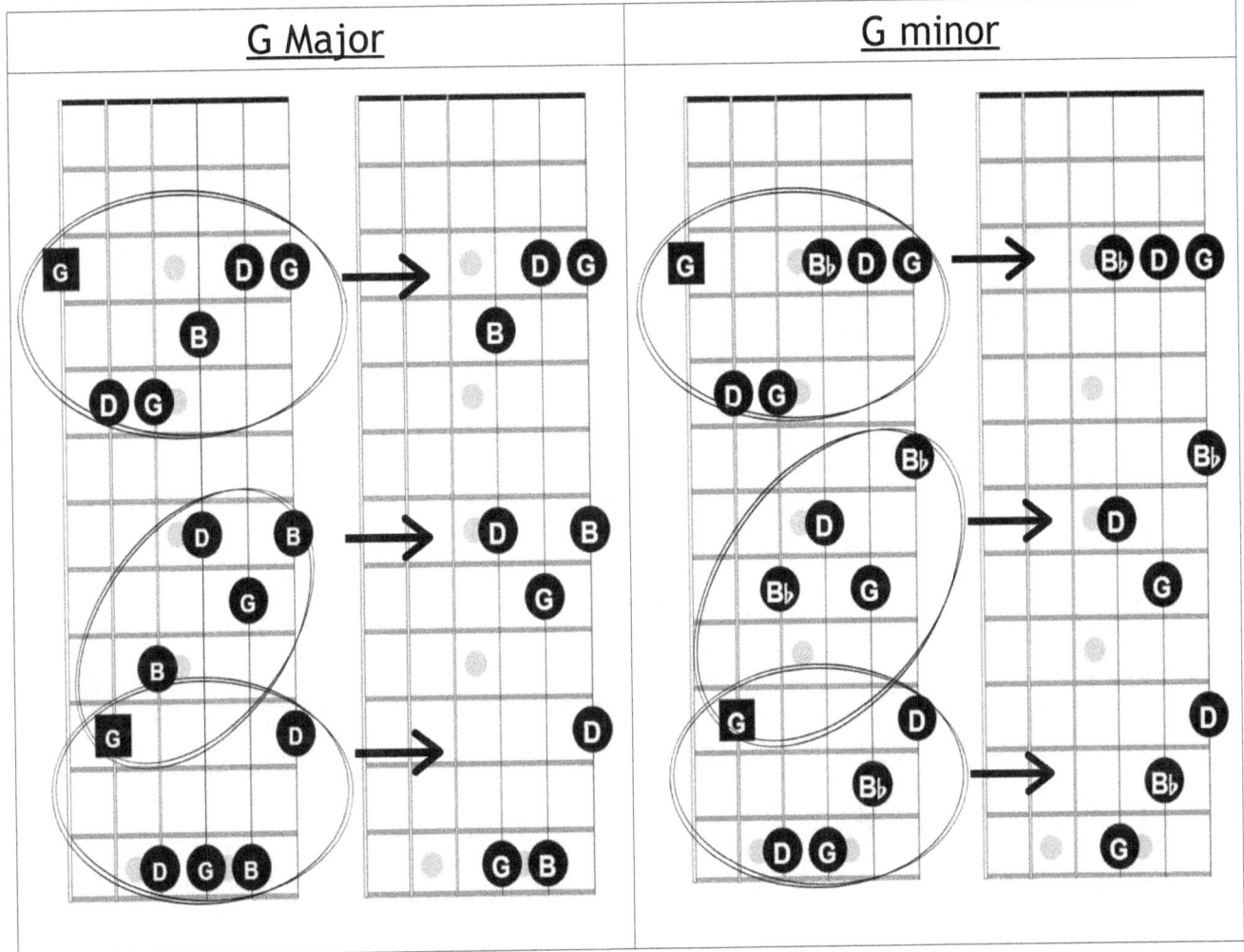

CHORD INVERSIONS GBE STRINGS

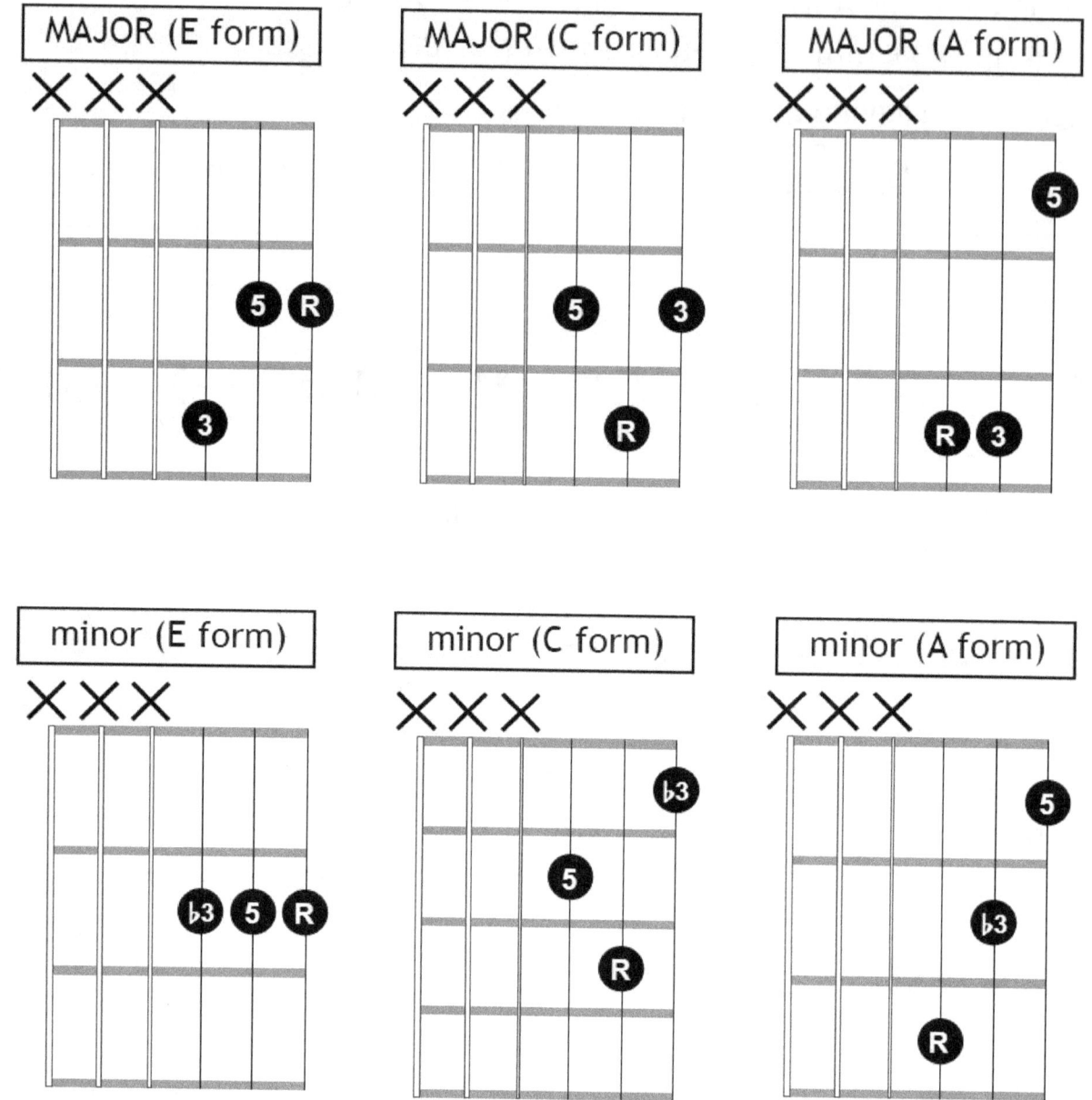

You can also memorize these according to where the ROOT is in each shape. I also found it easier to change from Major to minor when I could see the THIRD, the "toggle switch."

NOTE: The C and D shape chord shapes overlap. Some folks think of the C Shape as the D form.

WATCH CHORD INVERSIONS VIDEO at www.LeadGuitarWorkshop.com

PRACTICE

Chord Inversions for **G Em D C Am** (Ascend and descend each one)

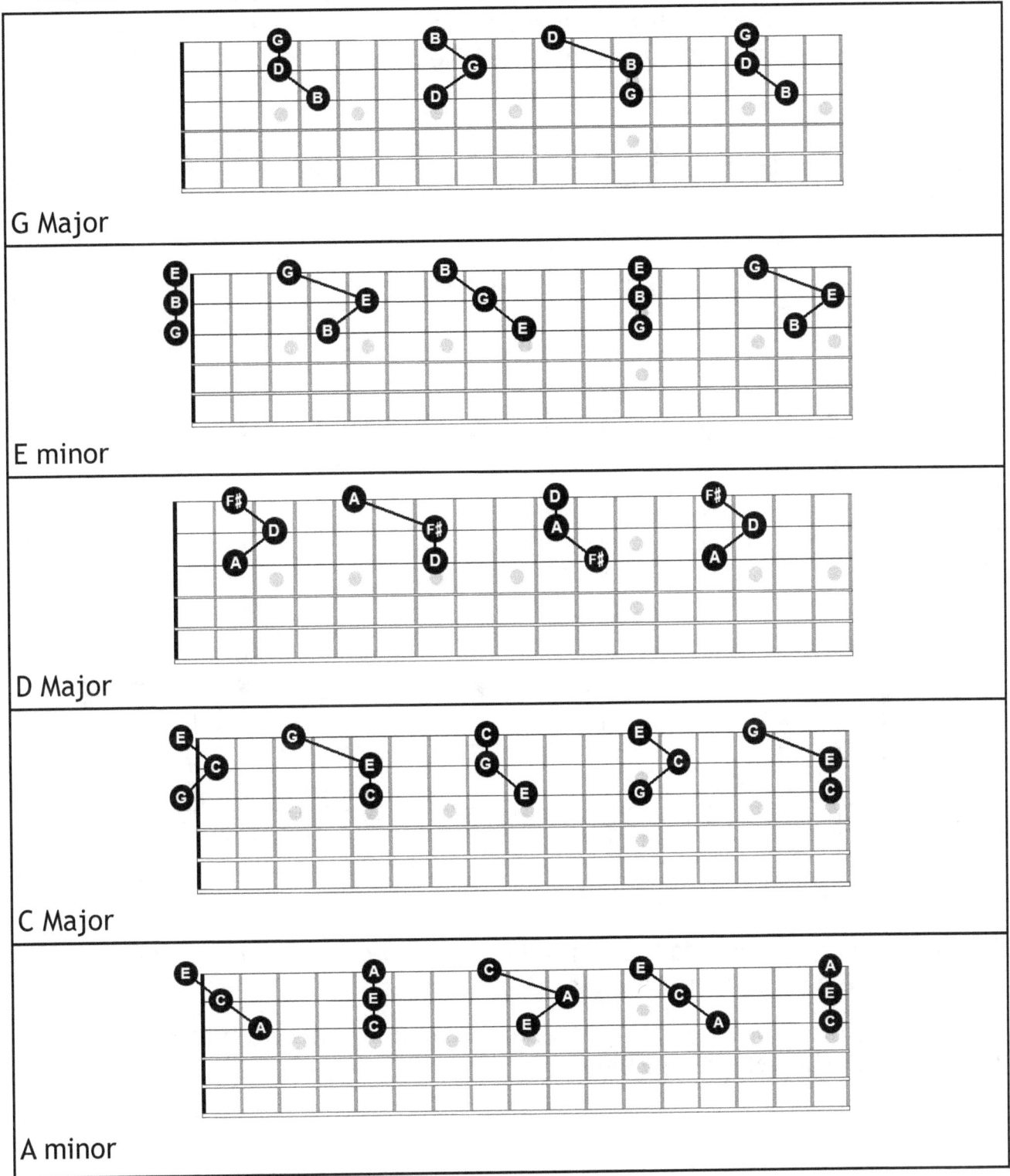

G Major

E minor

D Major

C Major

A minor

SELF-GEN

Here are some two bar self generations. Strum one bar of G and one bar of C and then strum one bar of G inversion and one bar C inversion. Usually you try to find the inversion that is the closest to the others.

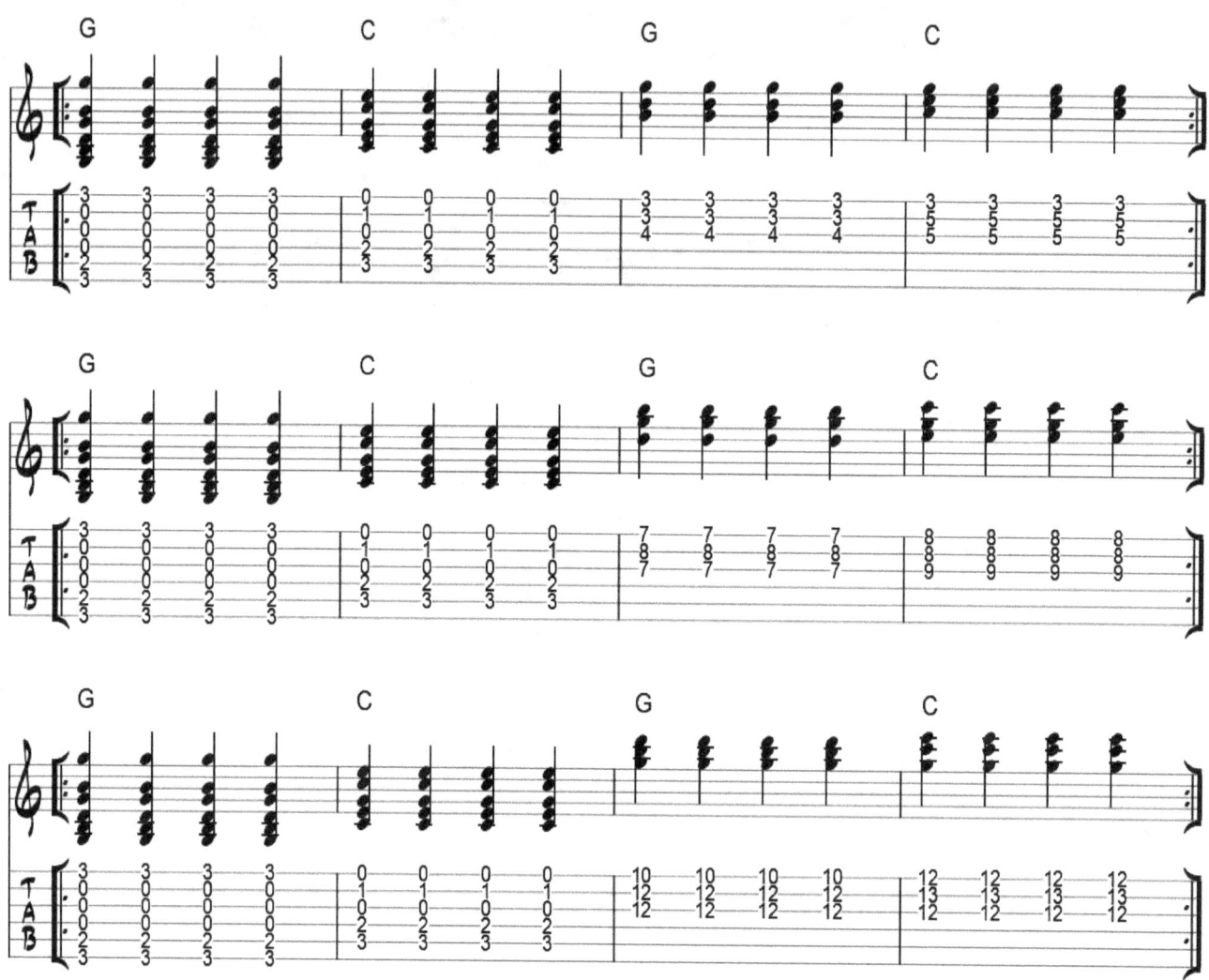

Pick any two chords and do the same. Find all three shapes for each chord. Then pair them up by which are closest.

Strum each chord (open or bar) for a bar each and then switch to the inversions for the second two bars.

SUMMARY

We are musicians and we are guitar players.

Music is Melody, Harmony, and Rhythm.

We think like a musician first and then go to our instrument.

We must always know the chords in our heads as we play.

THIRDS are the "Toggle Switch" in music, the ONLY thing dictating what is **Major** and what is **minor**. There are only 12 Major chords, and since we know the "toggle switch" we know the 12 minor chords too.

Know the Root, third and fifths of chords, as musicians and as guitar players. Start with the top 5 for guitar players. G C D Em and Am

Knowing the octave shapes on guitar is crucial to understanding your fretboard.

ABOVE, ACROSS AND BEHIND is one of the cleanest ways to look at arpeggios on the guitar neck, especially when you see them in your MODE patterns.

GUIDE TONES are one of the secrets of sounding great. They bridge the typical scale solo sound with the arpeggio sound, allowing you to "play the changes."

CHORD INVERSIONS are the gateways between rhythm guitar and lead guitar. They allow chords to move in different directions and they show you the chord tones.

CHAPTER 6

TUNE IN

"I am a musician and a guitar player. Music is my language and my guitar is my voice. Music is Melody, Harmony and Rhythm. I develop my language skills and my instrument skills. They are two separate worlds working together to complete the circle of music."

Rhythm is the number one factor to sounding great as a musician.

WARM UP

Muted String Ladder (MSL) 6 strings LEAPFROG all 4 gears

SHELL

Shell arpeggio using the ACROSS Major shape

ACROSS shape based on the G string is common when used as a Major arpeggio.
Navigate the ROOT note on the G string playing the NATURAL notes up and down. In SHELL fashion, play the arpeggios R35 ascending and descending and then REVERSE the order 53R and do it again.

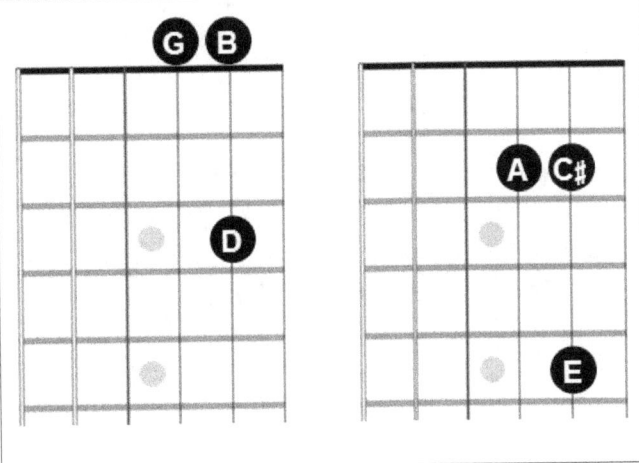

EXERCISE

Above Across and Behind in pattern # 3   **Key of G Major**   **Start 5ᵗʰ fret**

Am *Above*   Bm Behind   C *Behind*   D *Across*

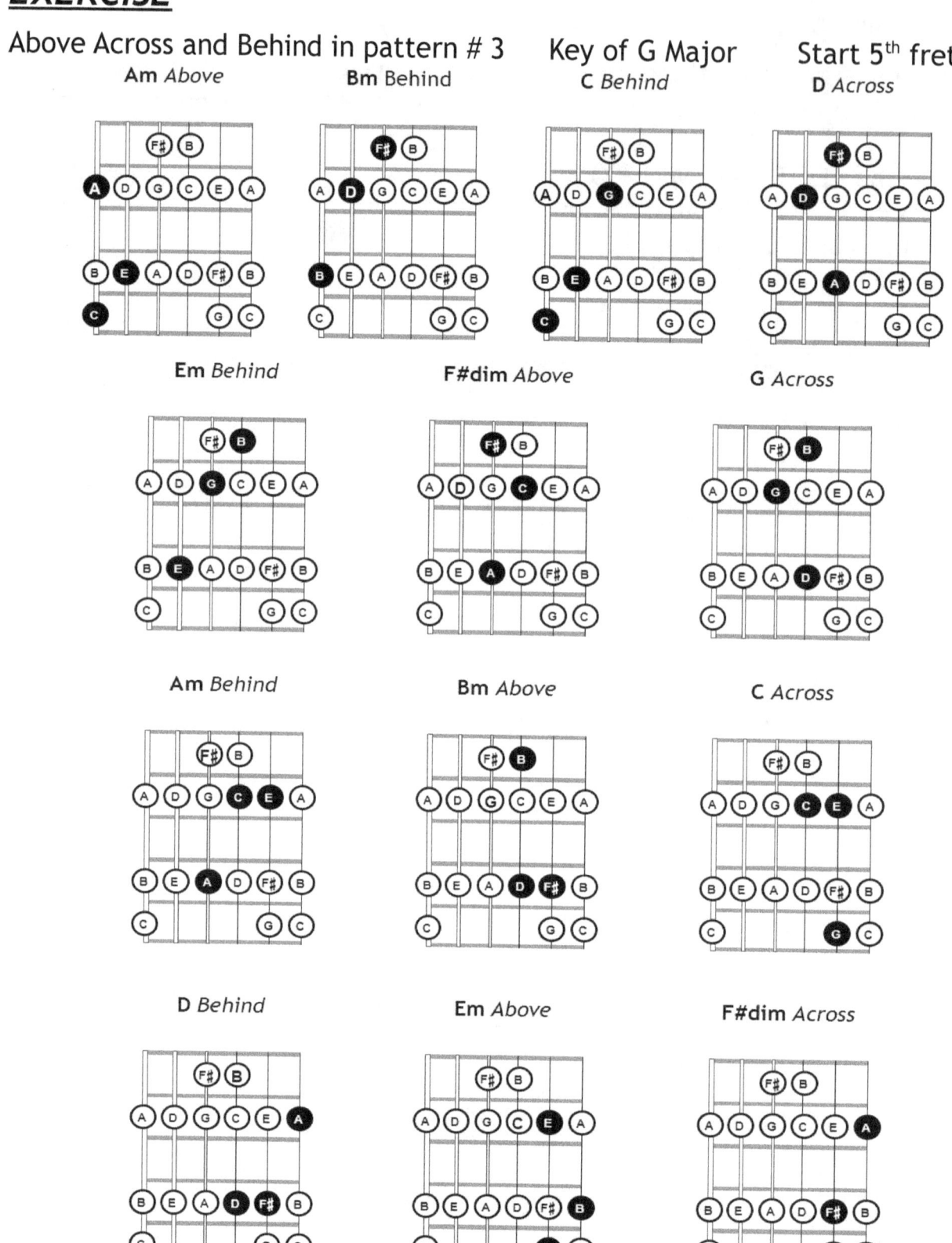

Em *Behind*   F#dim *Above*   G *Across*

Am *Behind*   Bm *Above*   C *Across*

D *Behind*   Em *Above*   F#dim *Across*

REVIEW

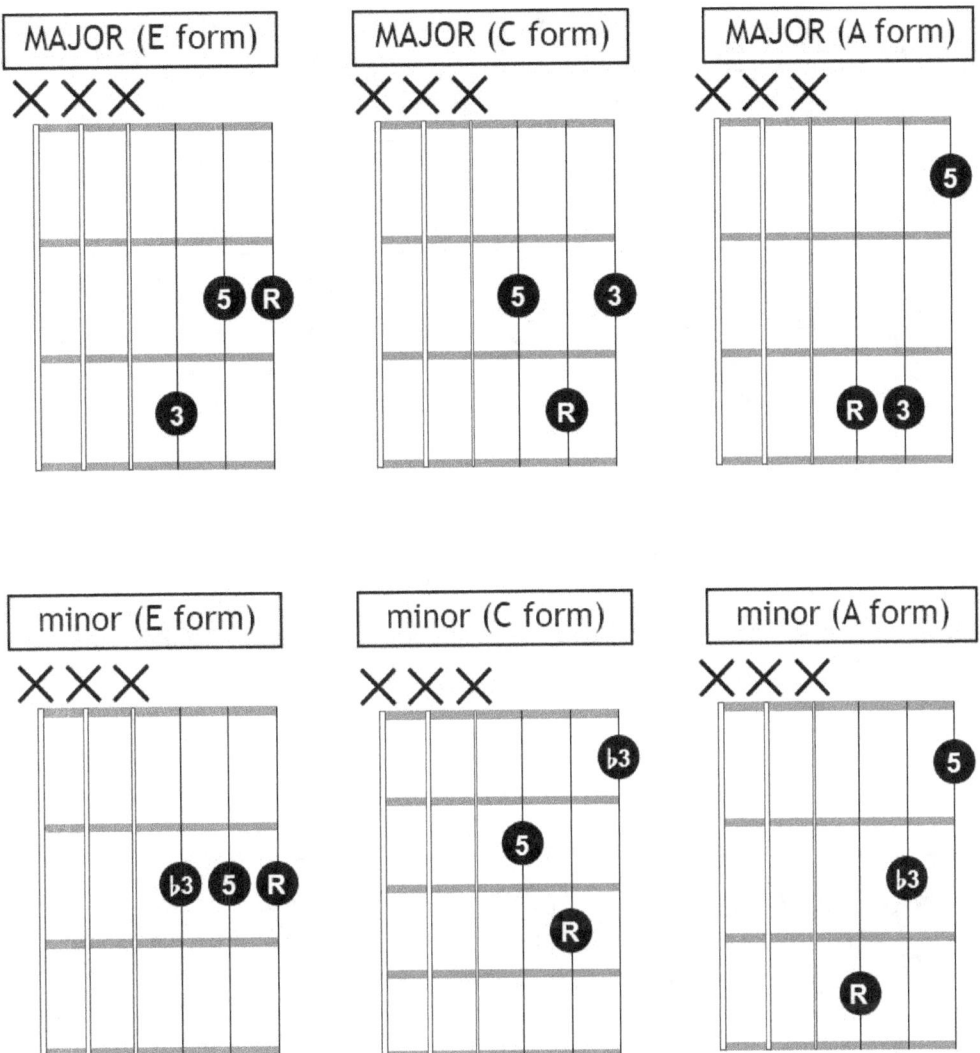

HOW TO PRACTICE

- Pick one of the top 5 chords (G C D Em Am) and navigate all three shapes plus an octave higher than the first shape (12 frets higher).
- Play each shape in time, either as whole-notes, half-notes or quarter-notes. Ascend and descend.
- Play them **POLYPHONIC** and **MONOPHONIC**. Think of them as little chord shapes AND as three notes to be played individually just like a scale. When you play them MONOPHONIC <u>do not hold the chord shape down</u>. Lift each finger for each note.

Chord Inversions for G Em D C Am

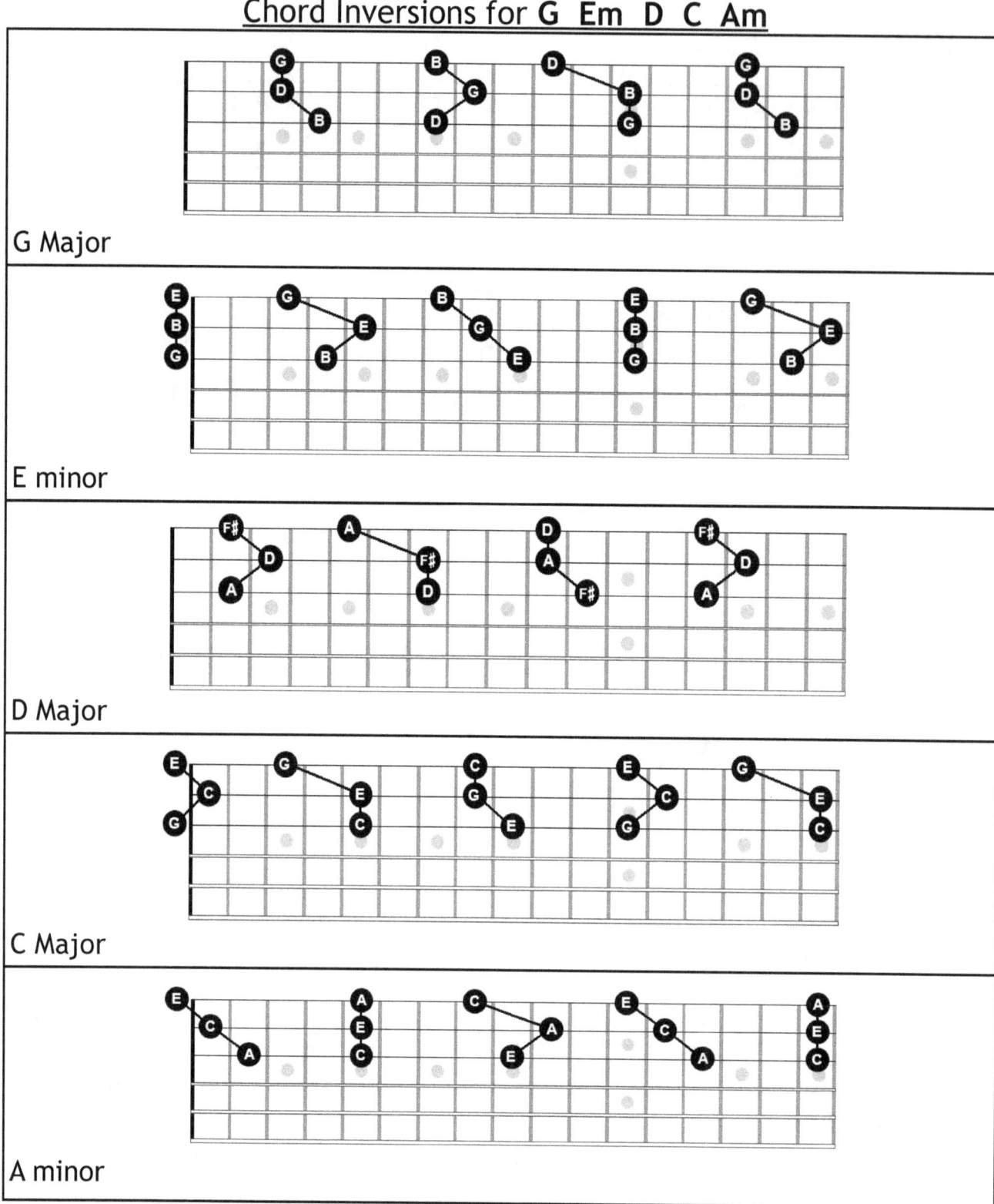

G Major

E minor

D Major

C Major

A minor

<u>NOTE:</u> Relatives (G/Em, C/Am) are only one note different. You can see this in the diagrams. G/Em difference is D to E and for C/Am it's G to A (5th going to the 6th of scale). This is a musical truth, not just guitar.

CHORD INVERSIONS part 2 DGB STRINGS

Using the same three chord shapes E C and A we can extract another group of inversions on the D G and B strings. These shapes are extremely common for rhythm guitar. These were the missing links to so many songs and they filled in a huge void in my chord vocabulary. I've included my nicknames for them.

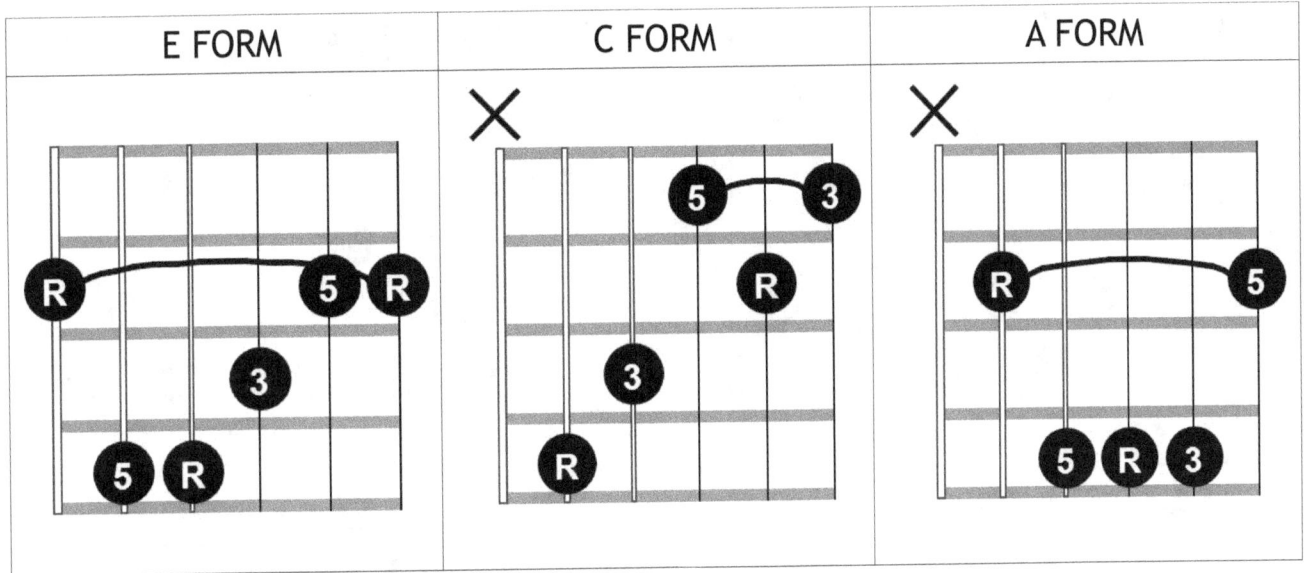

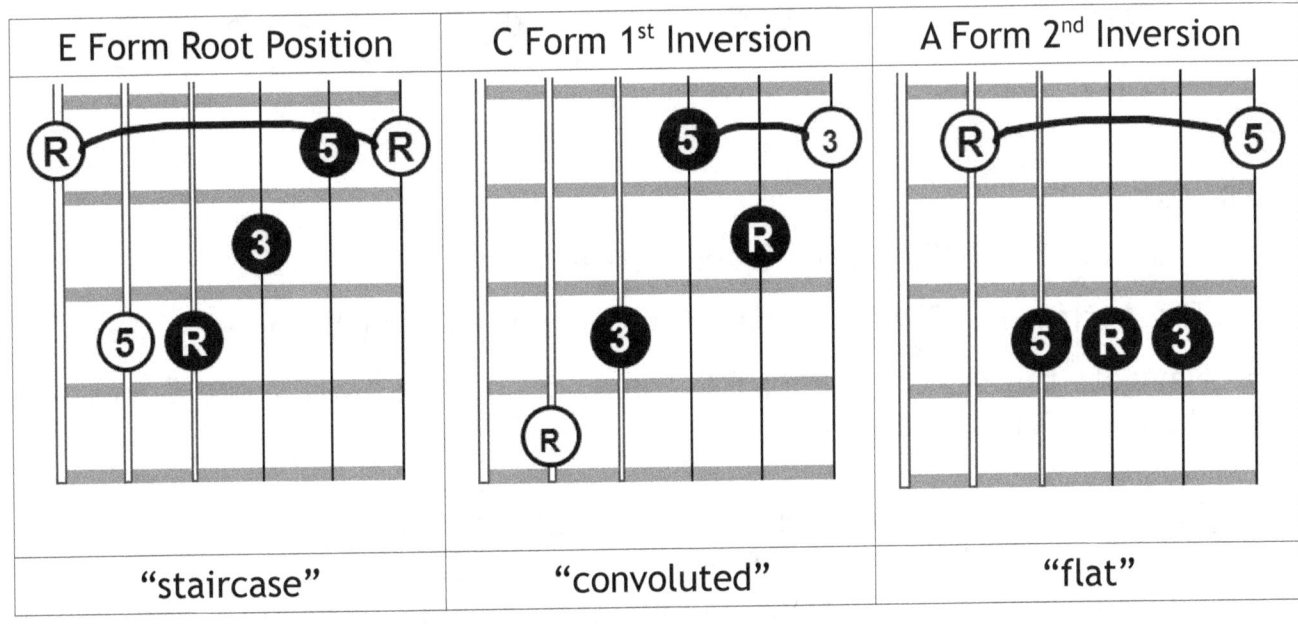

E Form Root Position	C Form 1st Inversion	A Form 2nd Inversion
"staircase"	"convoluted"	"flat"

Here are the E C A shapes for G Major and G minor on the DGB strings.

G Major	G minor

REMEMBER

- First find the ROOT on the E and A strings.
- The A string ROOT will be shared between the C and A shapes
- Navigate the 3 chord shapes E C and A. (E on the 6th string and C and A on the A string)

IMPORTANT: To maintain the sound of INVERSIONS it is really important to stay on the same groups of strings, DGB or GBE. Once you start crossing and combining, notes start duplicating and you start to play all of the notes again, reducing the ability of the inversion to move up and down in sound.

WATCH CHORD INVERSIONS VIDEO at www.LeadGuitarWorkshop.com

PRACTICE

SELF-GEN: Pick one chord and play each inversion for one bar. You can play them as whole-notes, half-notes, or quarter-notes.

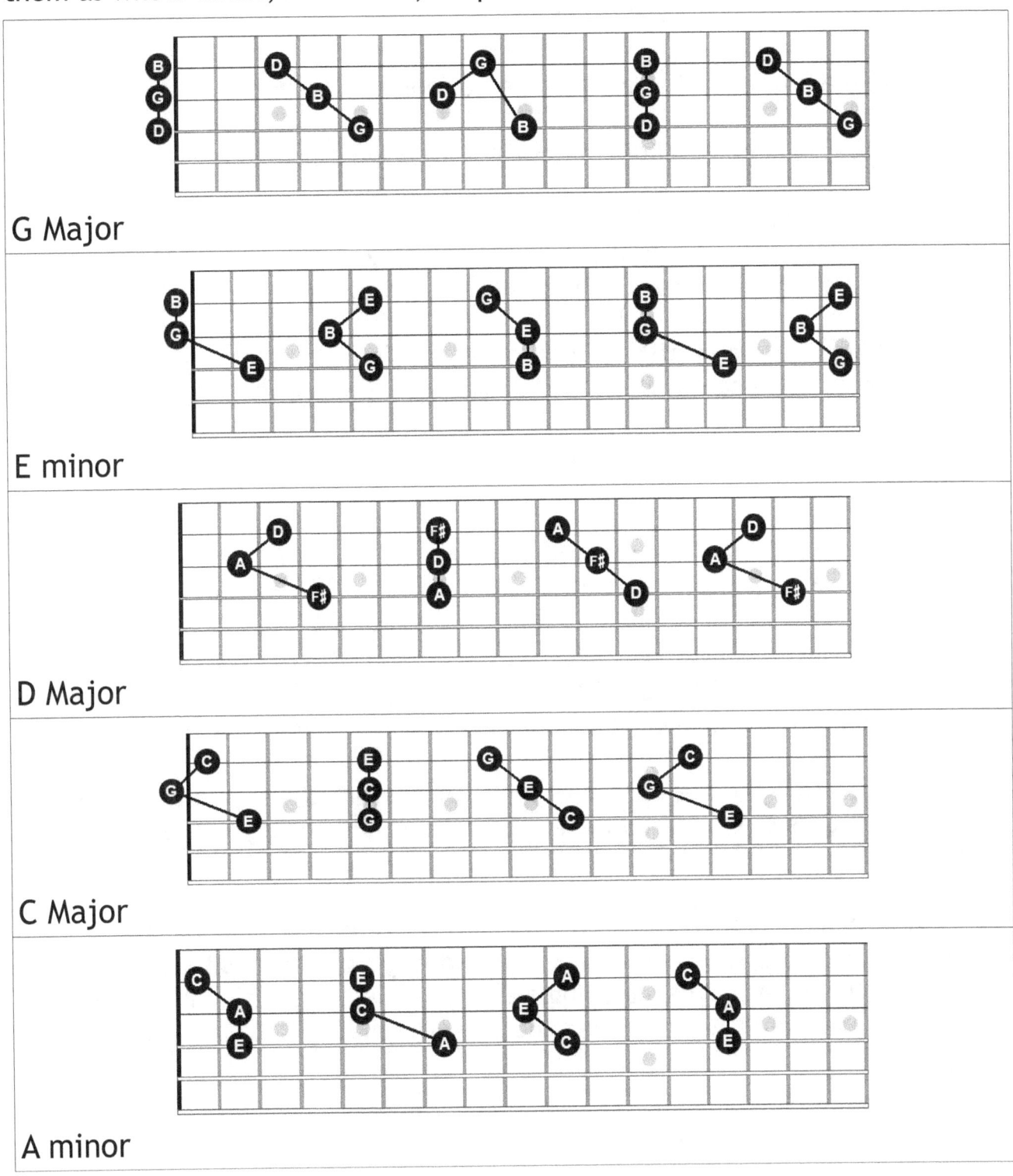

G Major

E minor

D Major

C Major

A minor

SUMMARY

We are musicians and we are guitar players.

Music is Melody, Harmony, and Rhythm.

We think like a musician first and then go to our instrument.

We must always know the chords in our heads as we play.

THIRDS are the "Toggle Switch" in music, the ONLY thing dictating what is **Major** and what is **minor**. There are only 12 Major chords, and since we know the "toggle switch" we know the 12 minor chords too.

Know the Root, third and fifths of chords, as musicians and as guitar players. Start with the most commonly used chords: G C D Em and Am.

Knowing the octave shapes on guitar is crucial to understanding your fretboard.

ABOVE, ACROSS AND BEHIND is one of the cleanest ways to look at arpeggios on the guitar neck, especially when you see them in any of your MODE patterns.

GUIDE TONES are one of the secrets of sounding great. They bridge the typical scale solo sound with the arpeggio sound, allowing you to "play the changes."

CHORD INVERSIONS are the gateways between rhythm guitar and lead guitar. They allow chords to move in different directions and show you the chord tones.

It's important to remember to keep INVERSIONS on the same strings to maintain their ability to move. If you keep adding more strings back into an inversion you will get back to playing all 5 or 6 strings, resulting in all the notes of all the chords all the time. That is very limiting in sound and enjoyment.

CHAPTER 7

TUNE IN

"I am a musician and a guitar player. Music is my language and my guitar is my voice. Music is Melody, Harmony and Rhythm. I develop my language skills and my instrument skills. They are two separate worlds working together to complete the circle of music."

Rhythm is the number one factor to sounding great as a musician.

WARM UP

Muted String Ladder (MSL)

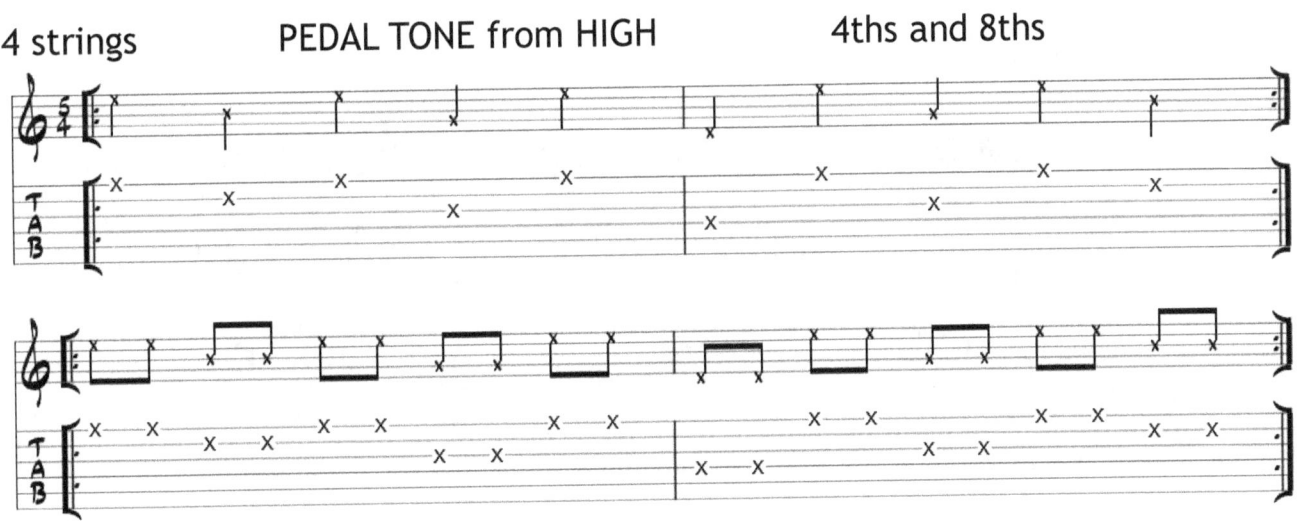

EXERCISE

Above Across and Behind in pattern #4 starting from 7th fret

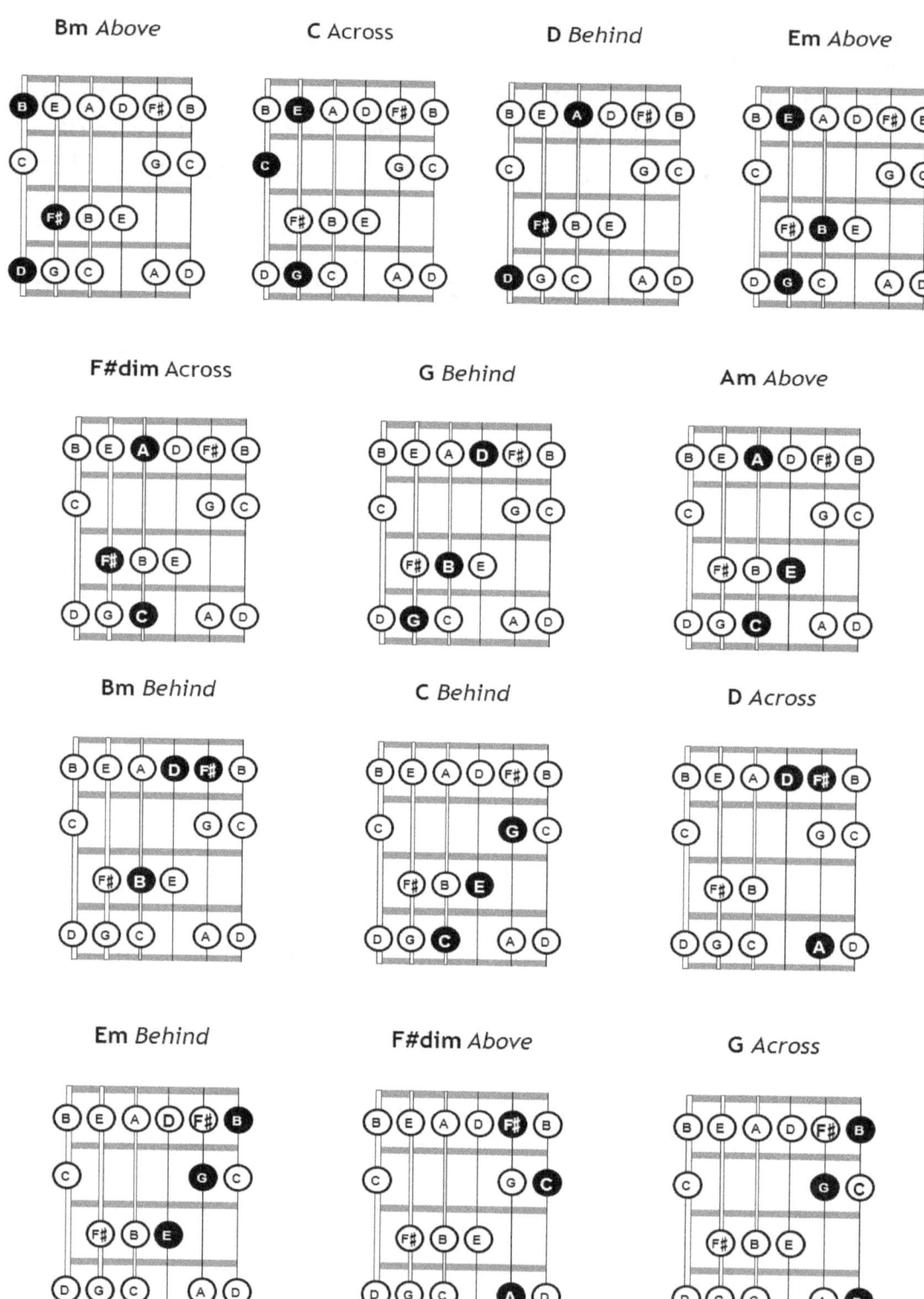

SELF-GEN: Pick one chord and play each inversion for one bar. You can play them as whole-notes, half-notes, or quarter-notes.

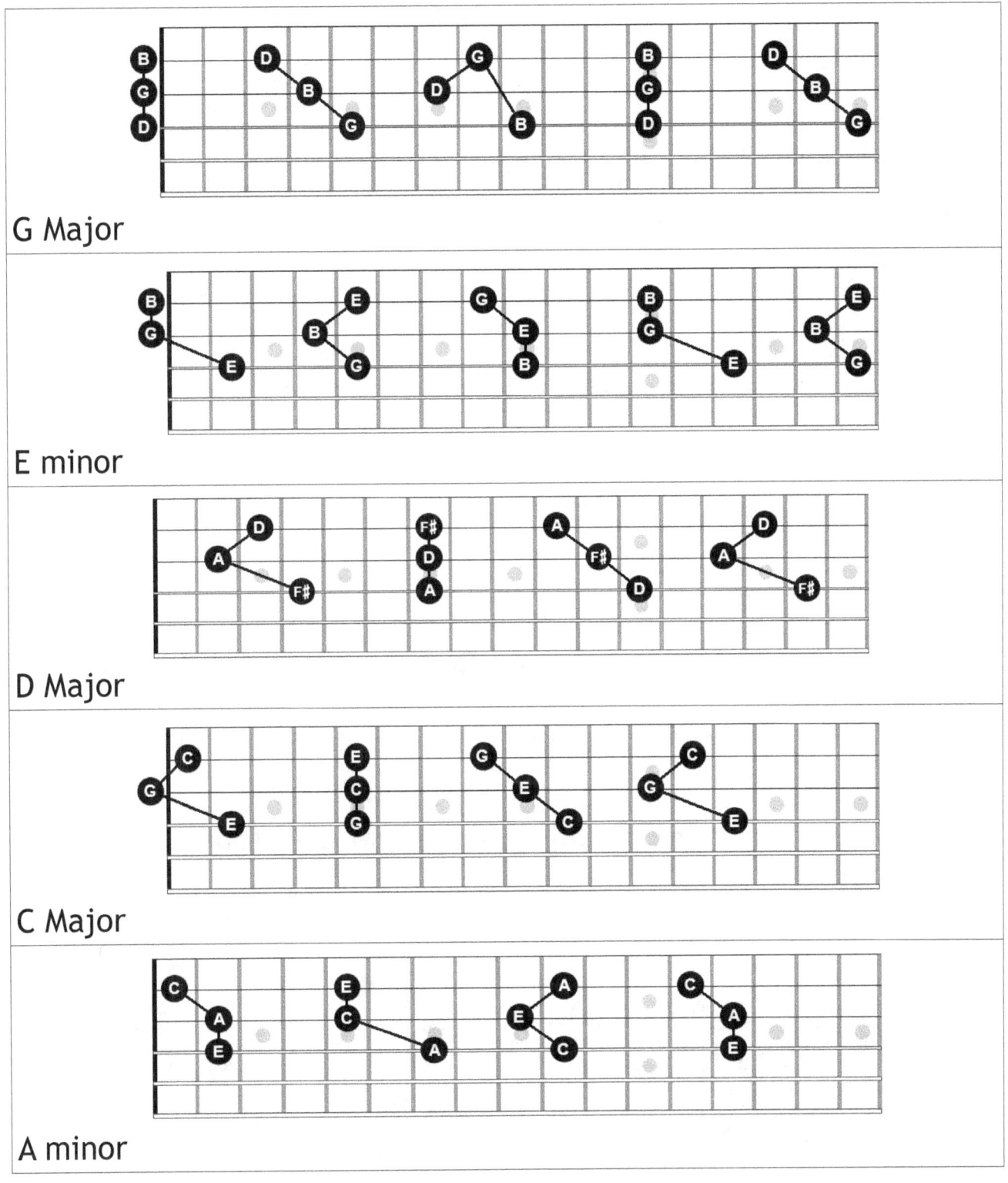

G Major

E minor

D Major

C Major

A minor

CHORD INVERSIONS REVIEW

Chord inversions completely reinvented chords and rhythm guitar concepts for me. The inversions were all the missing pieces to my guitar vocabulary. They were all the missing shapes in so many songs I was trying to learn (classic rock to Van Halen). They equally helped me accompany and solo.

Once you are comfortable with moving the inversions around for one chord, the next idea is to play multiple chords and staying in the same position (pattern). This results in great voice leading.

When you play I IV and V chords in position they will each use one of the 3 inversion shapes.

Here is G, C and D in pattern #2 with GBE string inversion shapes.

G   C   D

Here is G, C and D in pattern #2 with DGB string inversion shapes.

G   C   D

Lead Guitar Chords and Arpeggios   CHAPTER 7

The same is true with the 3 minor chords.

Here is Em, Am and Bm in pattern #2 with the GBE string inversion shapes.

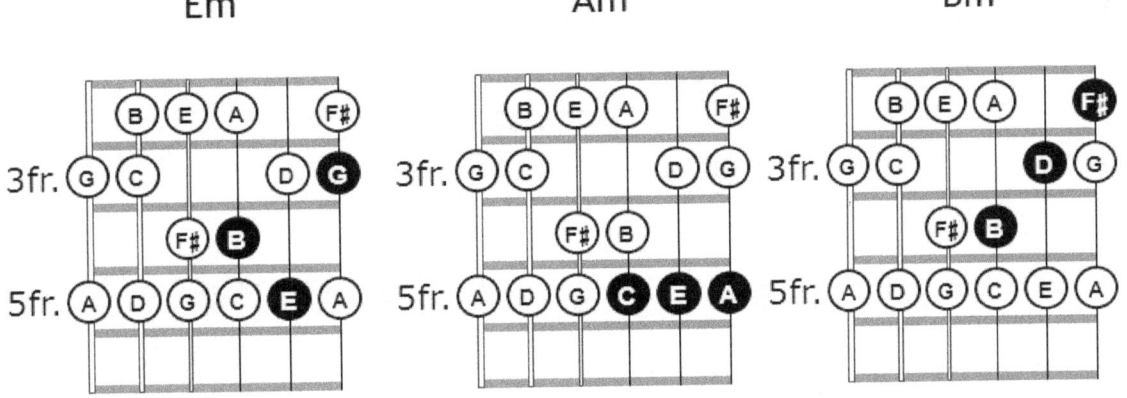

Here is Em, Am and Bm in pattern #2 with the DGB string inversion shapes. Note: The Am requires you to reach into pattern #3. There is usually one chord that needs to extend to the next pattern.

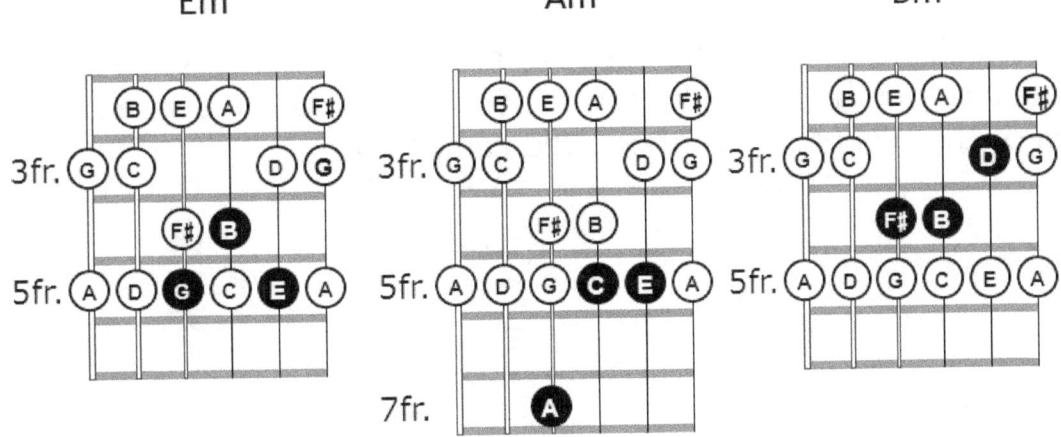

It's remarkable to think that in any one of the five mode patterns we can play all seven chords in more than one way. This adds a tremendous amount of opportunity to expand your sound and abilities.

Here is G D Em and C with chord inversions played in position on the GBE and DGB strings. This is smooth voice leading.

Inversions also allow you the incredible power to make it go in the opposite direction of the chords and elongate a chord progression. (That's cool!)

Here is an example of going the opposite direction. When playing and A to a G chord, the A sounds higher and the G lower. But, if you use a different inversion of the G chord, then the sound can go up.

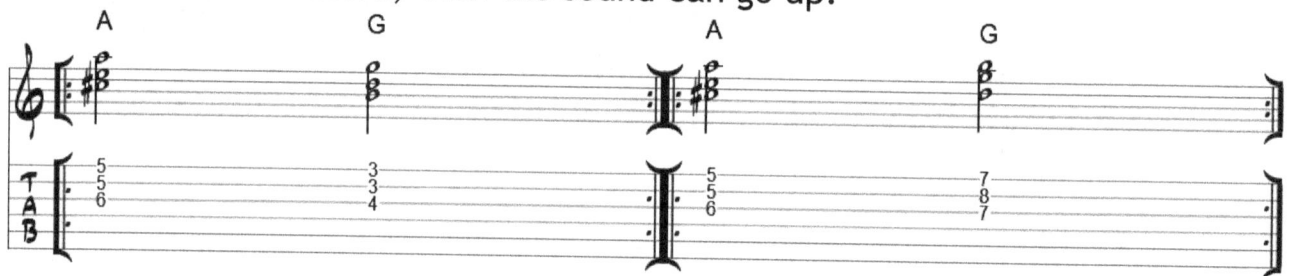

You can also elongate the progression (turning it from a 1 bar to 2 bar sound).

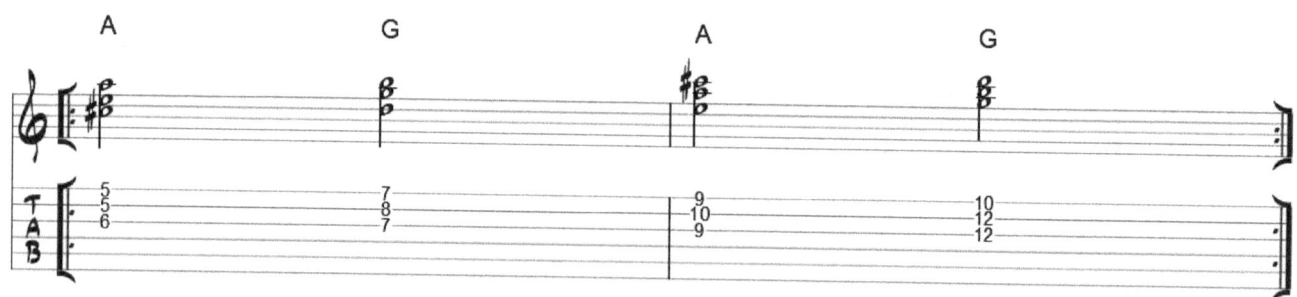

It is also extremely valuable to learn to play the inversions as monophonic sounds. One note-at-a-time and not holding down a shape like it is a chord. Think of it as a 3 note scale. You can sing it and play it, one note-at-a-time.

Here is a G major chord and A minor chord with each of their inversions as single notes. There is no set way as to how to play the notes. They are in the scale patterns and can be landed on as you solo to line up with the chord. You can also just trace the shapes and use them as mini scales that only have chord tones.

Same idea with G D Em C chord progression. Be creative as to how you play them.

CAGED SYSTEM

CAGED is a common tool for guitar players. It's not a sound and is only an instrumental benefit for guitar players. The basic idea is that you can map out the 12 fret fretboard with 5 shapes. Each shape is a chord and a scale pattern. It is a very useful system but for arpeggios you really just need to focus on the E C A shapes. There are only three notes in a triad and E C A shapes have them.

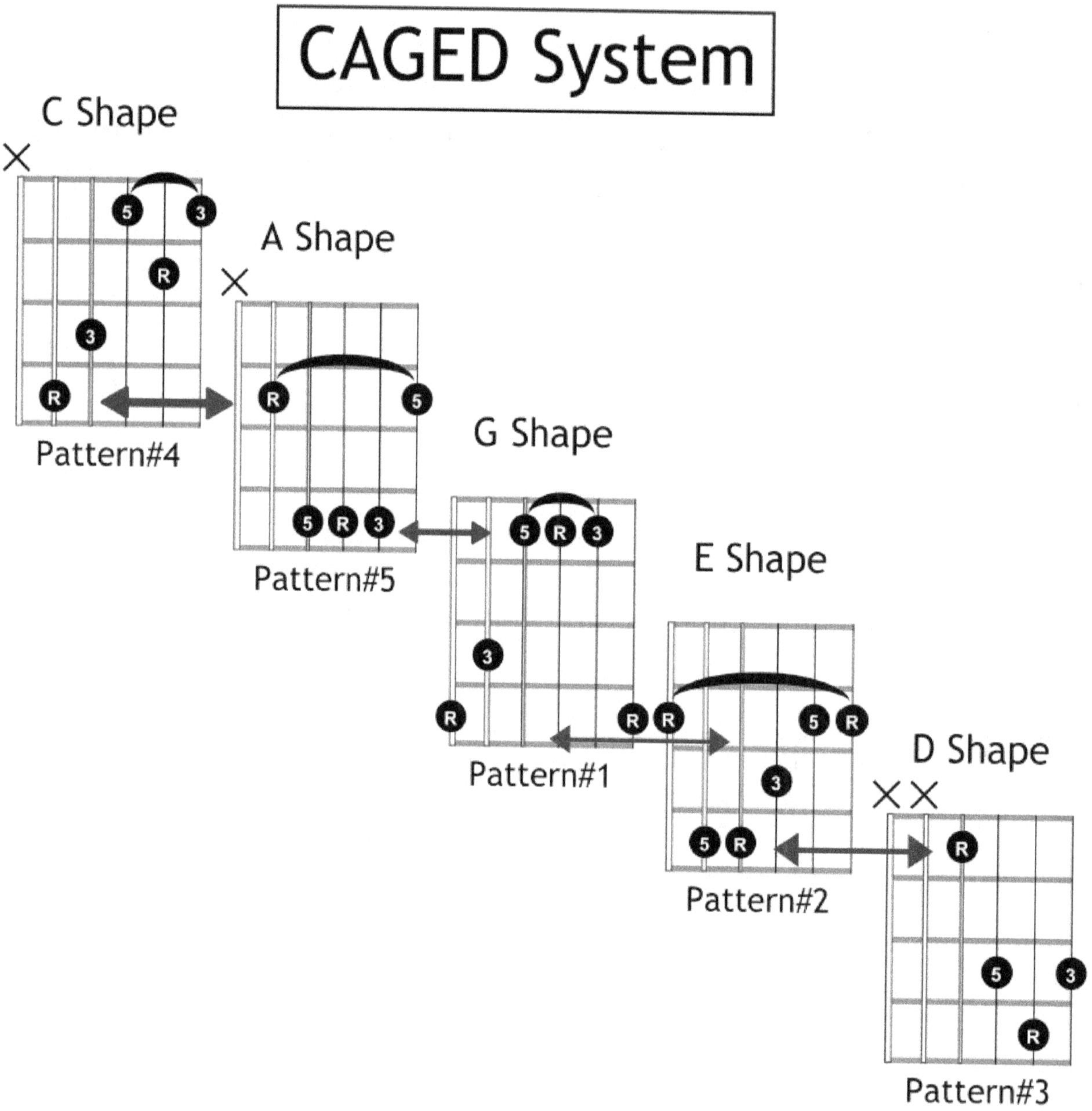

CAGED System

C Shape

Pattern#4

A Shape

Pattern#5

G Shape

Pattern#1

E Shape

Pattern#2

D Shape

Pattern#3

WATCH CAGED VIDEO at www.LeadGuitarWorkshop.com

E C A SHAPES

Here are the full arpeggios for the E C A shapes for G Major and G minor. You can look at this in many ways. You should see the pentatonic pattern and the chord shape sitting on top of it. You can see that there are two Above, Across, and Behind shapes per pattern. You can also see the chord inversions we looked at in the last two chapters. These can be used for Guide Tone lines, notes to highlight as you play the changes, sweeping, so many options.

G Major

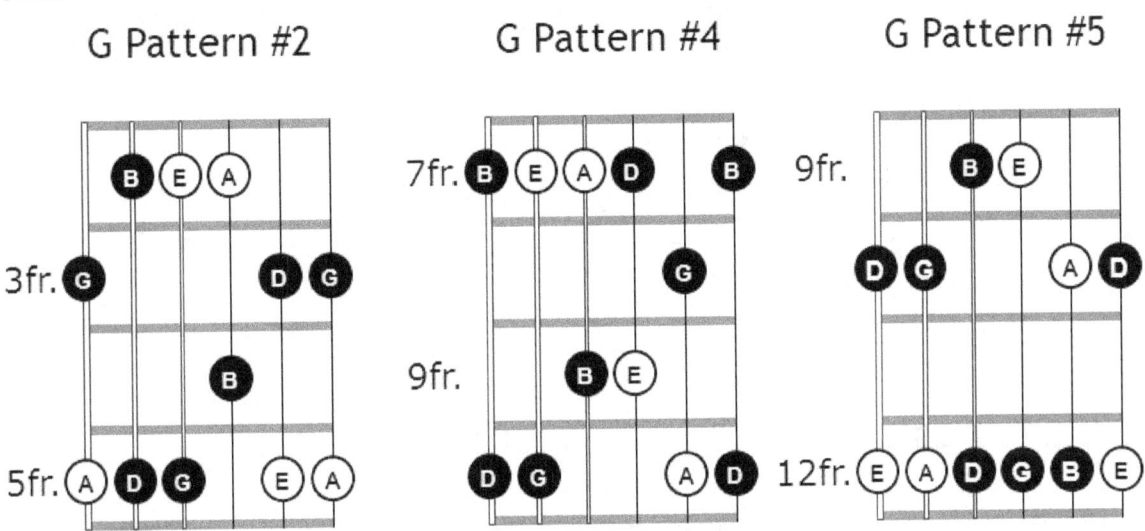

G minor

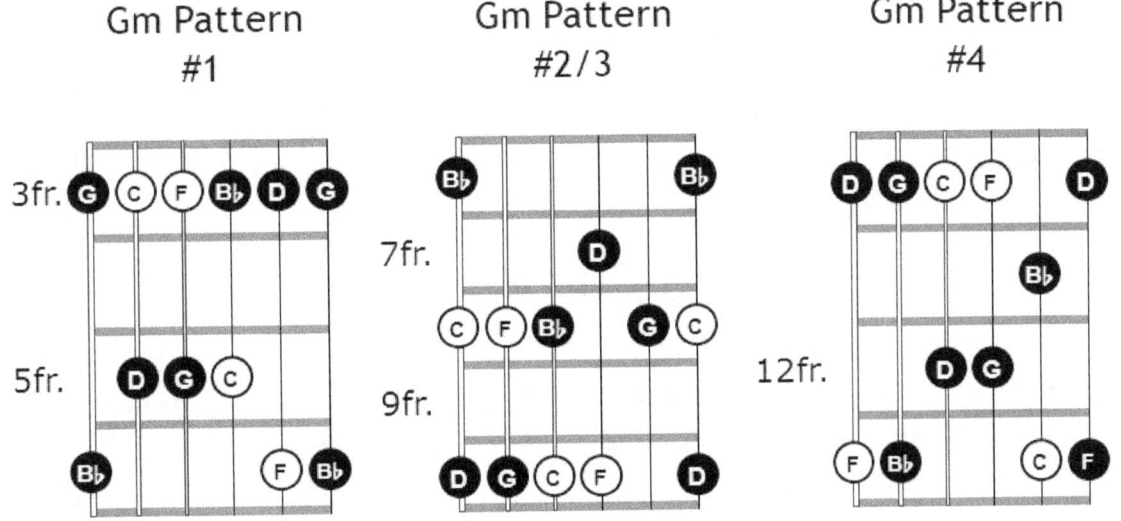

PRACTICE

E C A Shapes full pattern arpeggios for G Major

E C A Shapes full pattern arpeggios for G minor

SUMMARY

We are musicians and we are guitar players.

Music is Melody, Harmony, and Rhythm.

We think like a musician first and then go to our instrument.

We must always know the chords in our heads as we play.

Know the ROOT, THIRD and FIFTH of chords, as musicians and as guitar players. Start with the most commonly used chords: G C D Em and Am.

Knowing the OCTAVE SHAPES on guitar is crucial to understanding your fretboard.

ABOVE, ACROSS AND BEHIND is one of the cleanest ways to look at arpeggios on the guitar neck, especially when you see them in any of your MODE patterns.

GUIDE TONES are one of the secrets of sounding great. They bridge the typical scale solo sound with the arpeggio sound allowing you to "play the changes."

CHORD INVERSIONS are the gateways between rhythm guitar and lead guitar. They allow chords to move in different directions and show you the chord tones.

It's important to remember to keep INVERSIONS on the same strings to maintain their ability to move. If you keep adding more strings back into an inversion you will get back to playing all 5 or 6 strings, resulting in all the notes of all the chords all the time. That is very limiting in sound and enjoyment.

CAGED system is a guitar convention for the 5 shapes on our fretboard. For arpeggios we just need to focus on the E C A shapes to get the 3 notes and inversions.

CHAPTER 8

TUNE IN

"I am a musician and a guitar player. Music is my language and my guitar is my voice. Music is Melody, Harmony and Rhythm. I develop my language skills and my instrument skills. They are two separate worlds working together to complete the circle of music."

Rhythm is the number one factor to sounding great as a musician.

WARM UP

Muted String Ladder (MSL) 4 strings   PEDAL TONE from HIGH   All 4 gears

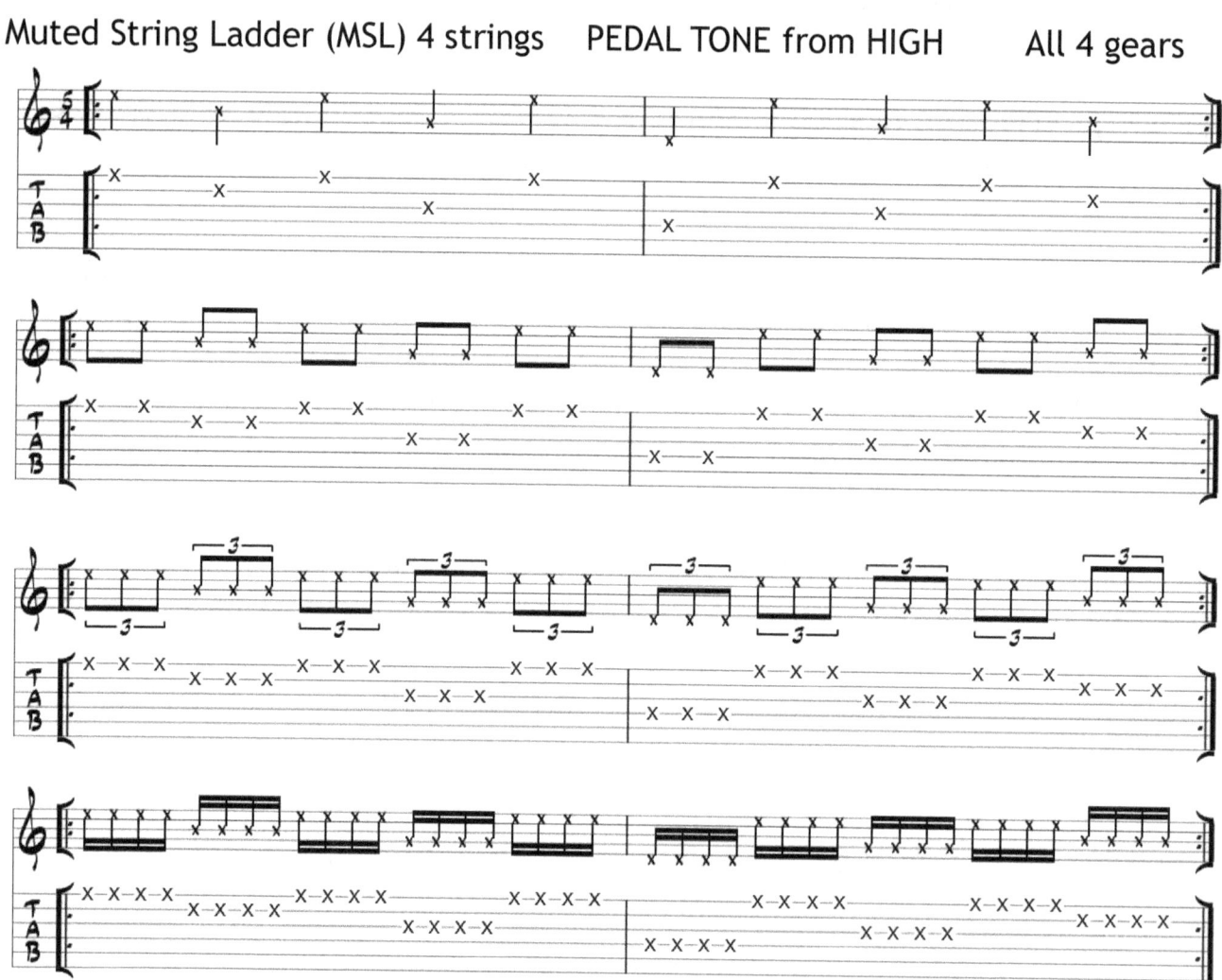

EXERCISE

Above Across and Behind in pattern #5 start 10th fret

| D *Across* | Em *Behind* | F#dim *Above* | G *Across* |

| Am *Behind* | Bm *Above* | C *Across* |

| D *Behind* | Em *Above* | F#dim *Across* |

| G *Behind* | Am *Above* | Bm *Across** |

Chord Inversions for G Am Bm C D Em in pattern #2 GBD and DBG

Play each inversion for one bar. You can strum or arpeggiate each chord. Try playing in the order of the Key (G, Am, Bm, C, D, Em). You can also play any chord progression in this key, including its modes. For example an A Dorian progression could be Am G D Am.

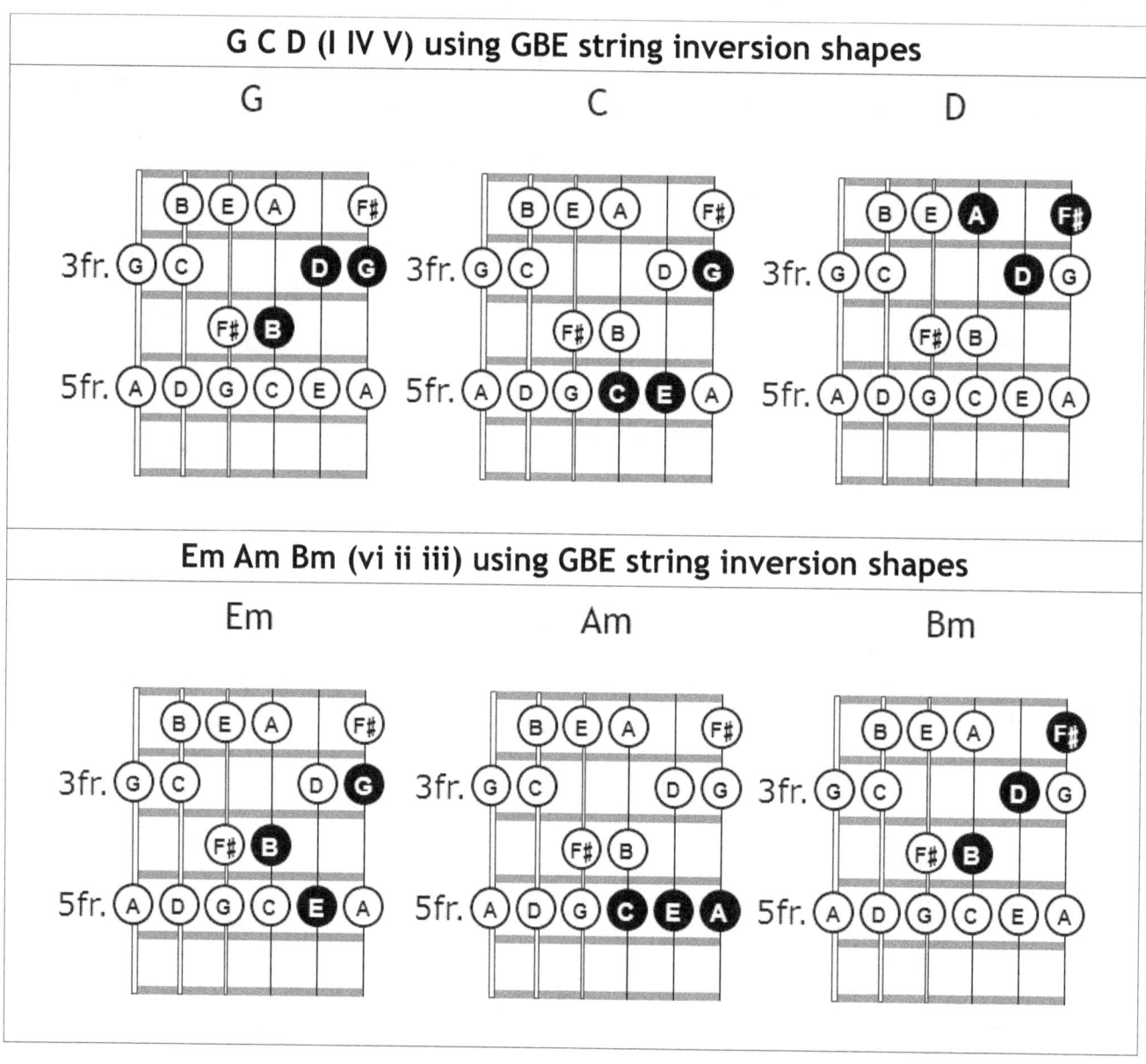

G C D (I IV V) using DGB string inversion shapes

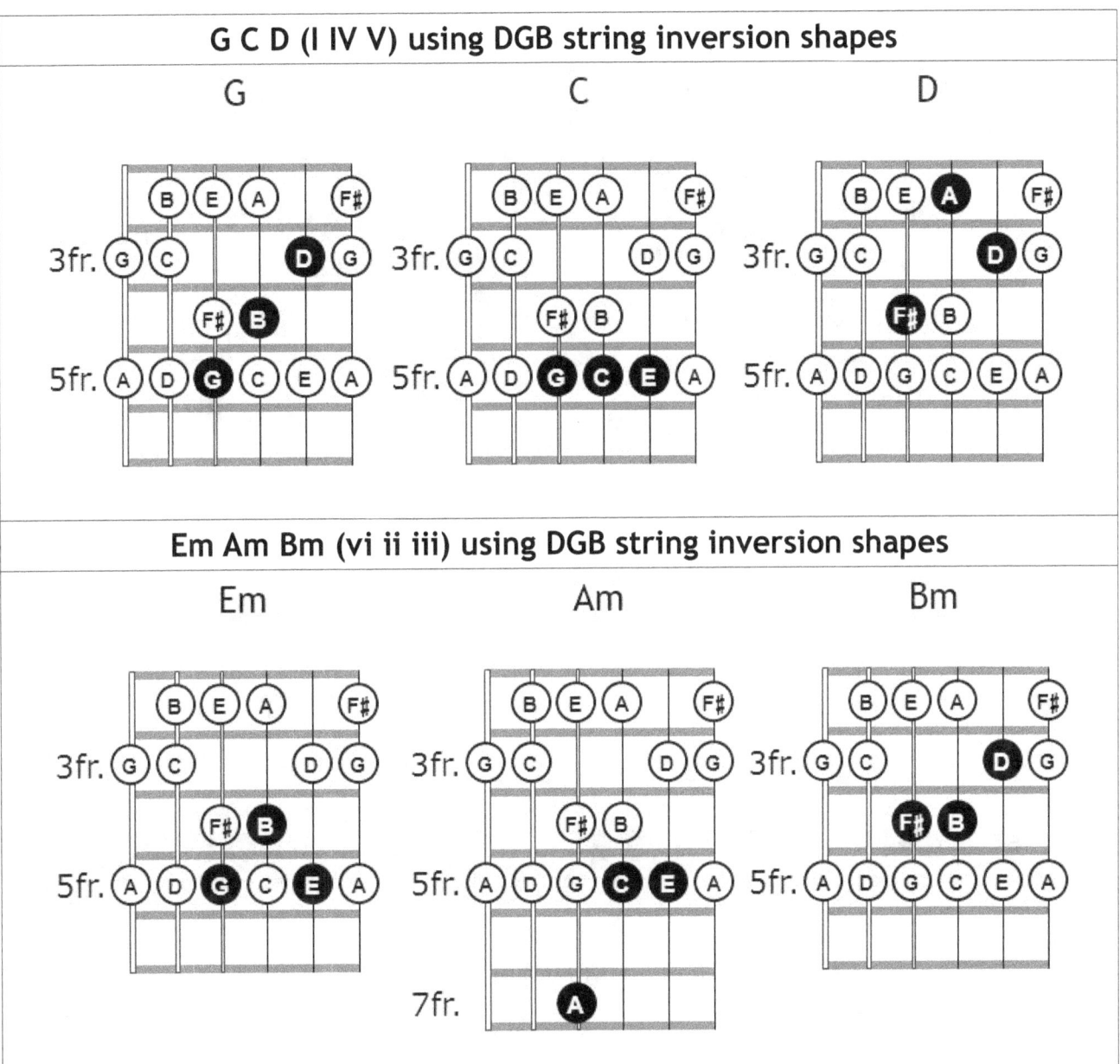

Em Am Bm (vi ii iii) using DGB string inversion shapes

E C A SHAPES REVIEW

E C A Shapes for G Major and G minor. Play each one note-at-a-time.

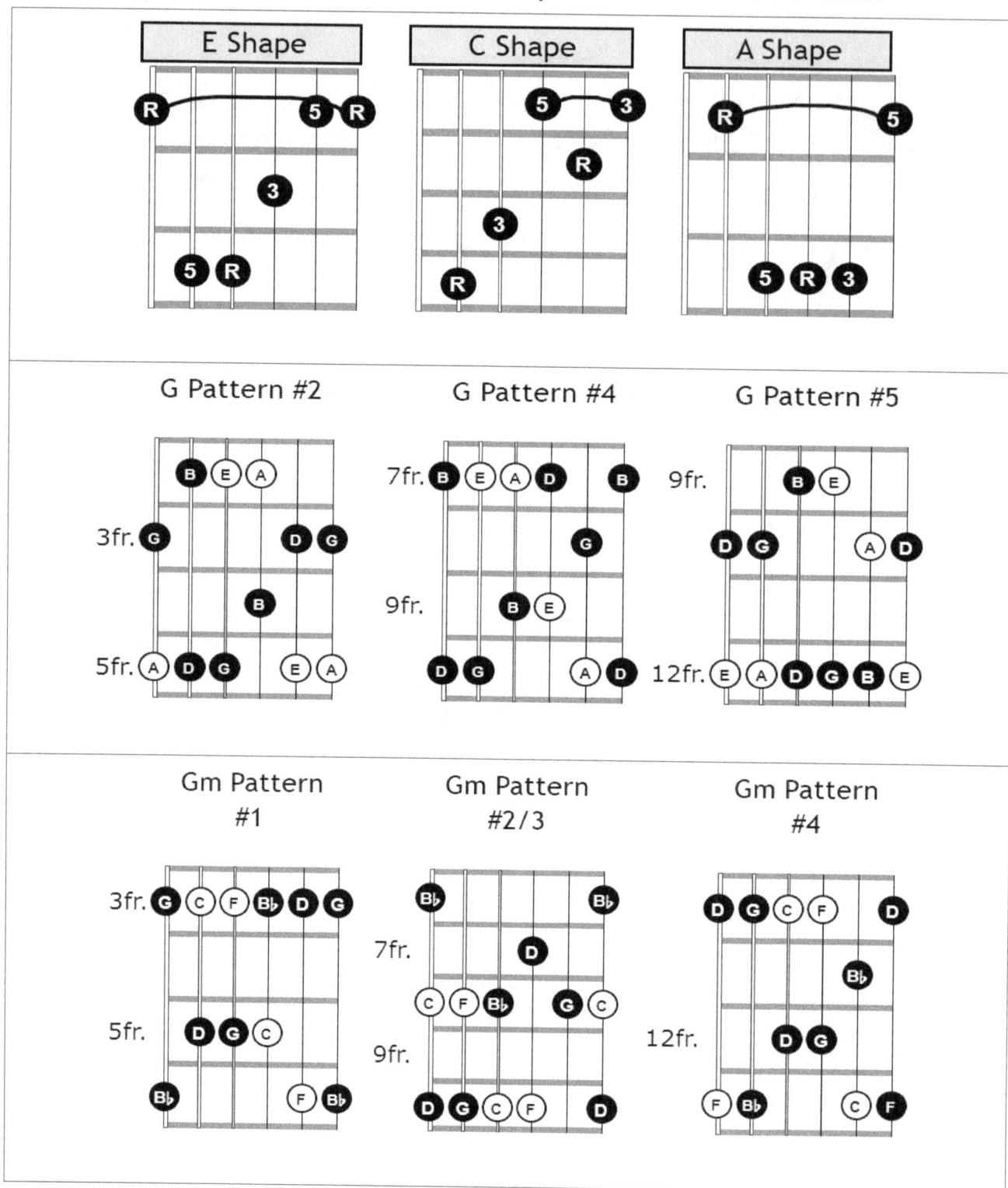

GUIDE TONE LINES REVIEW

Guide tone lines are a simple melody that uses chord tones to help provide a stable set of notes that you can build a solo/melody upon. Guide tone lines are in solos, backup vocals, strings, chord voicings, so many places.

As a musician you need to know the notes in each chord and be able to connect them to the next available chord tone by the smallest interval.

Here are two guide tone lines for G D Em C backing track.

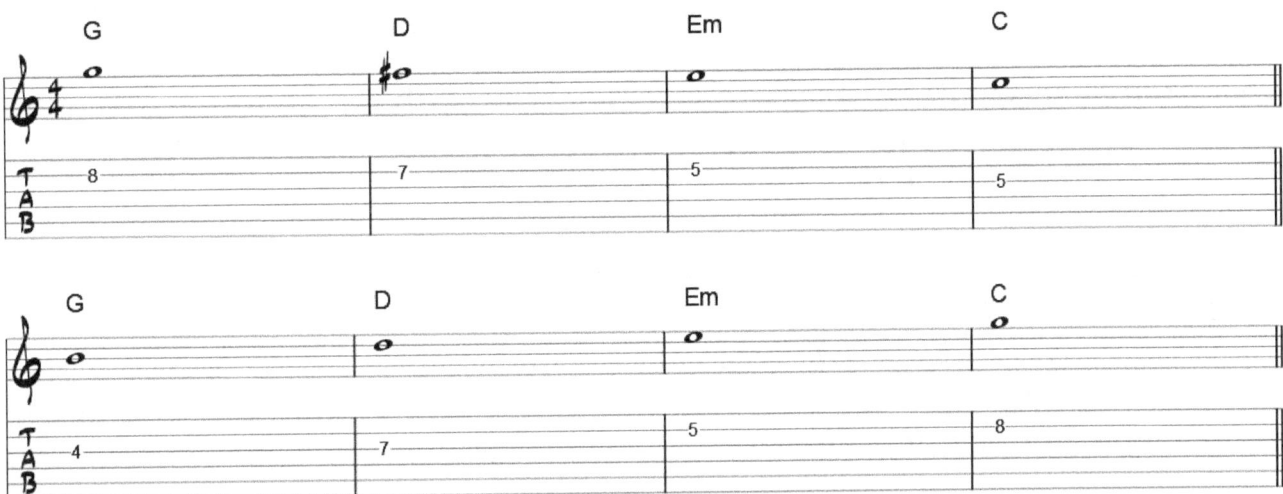

Here are two guide tone lines for Em D Am C backing track.

SECOND INVERSION ARPEGGIO

Chord inversions are just the order of the triad in one of its three combinations.

Root position	1st Inversion	2nd Inversion
5	R	3
3	5	R
R	3	5

We looked at this in detail as chord inversions but with the Above, Across and Behind in ROOT position. There are inversions of melodic arpeggios too. As you can imagine they can be overwhelming to navigate.

There is one shape that I see all the time and that is a SECOND INVERSION arpeggio in the ABOVE position. One of the things that makes this cool for a guitar player is the lowest two notes are a mini-bar. This shape happens most of the time on the top two strings. Here it is for Major and minor. The shape is the same on all strings EXCEPT the GB combination.

2nd INV Major   2nd INV minor

SMALL SWEEP ARPEGGIOS

Another place you will see second inversion arpeggios is in the the small sweep shapes. They happen on the upper three strings and use the ACROSS shape plus the 5th of the chord below it. This creates a second inversion arpeggio.

Economy/Sweep picking is when you pick in the same direction and use the same motion. You let the pick land on the next string before you strike. It should be one fluid motion, not multiple plucks. It can be down and up.

These are six note phrases. It is often played with 16th note triplets (6th gear). It is written below in 8th note triplets and 16th note triplets. These are equally at home as 8th notes and 16th notes even though they are six notes. They sound really cool as they overlap the beat and cause an unresolved tension that perpetuates motion.

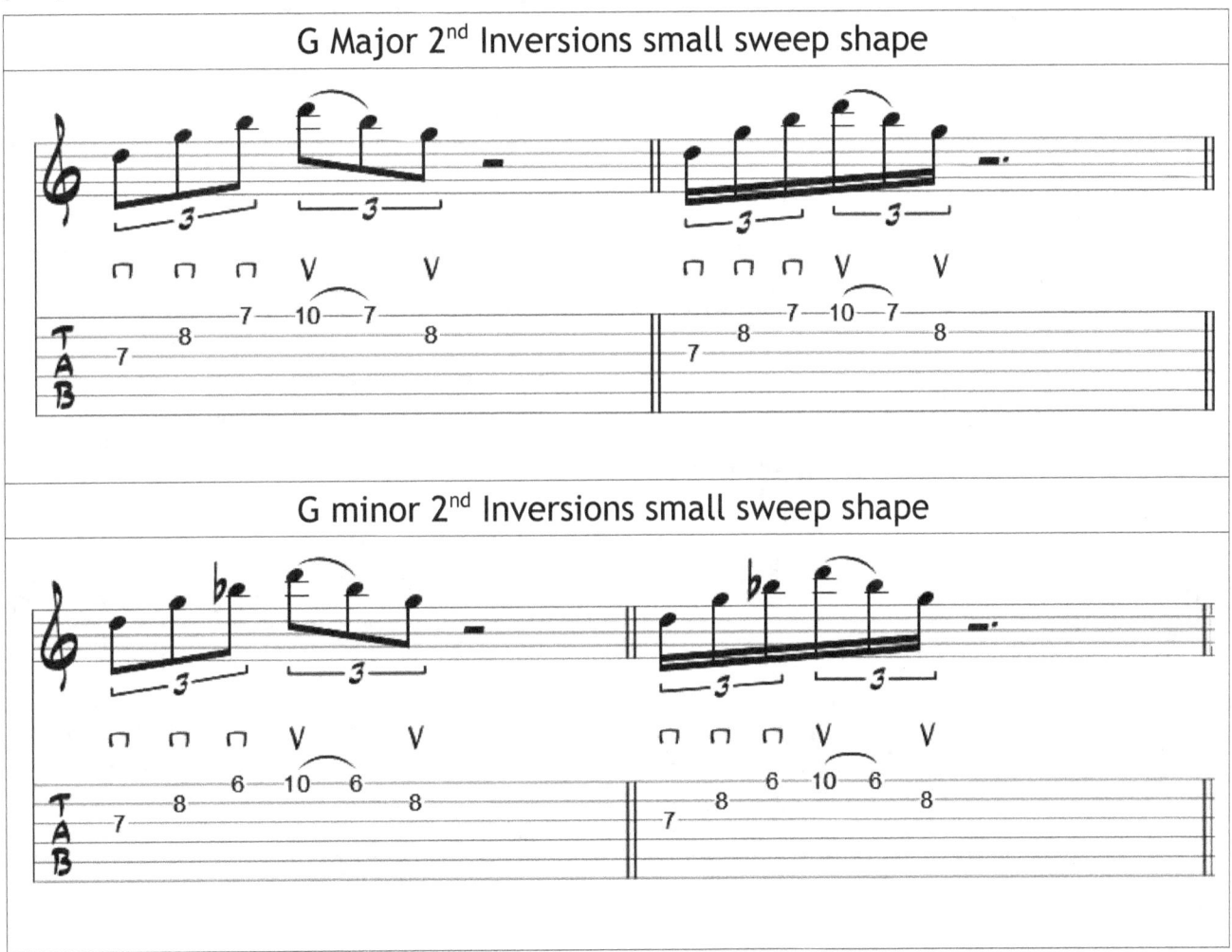

PRACTICE

Here is the G D Em C progression with each chord arpeggiated with a Tresillo. The D and Em shapes use the 2nd Inversion.

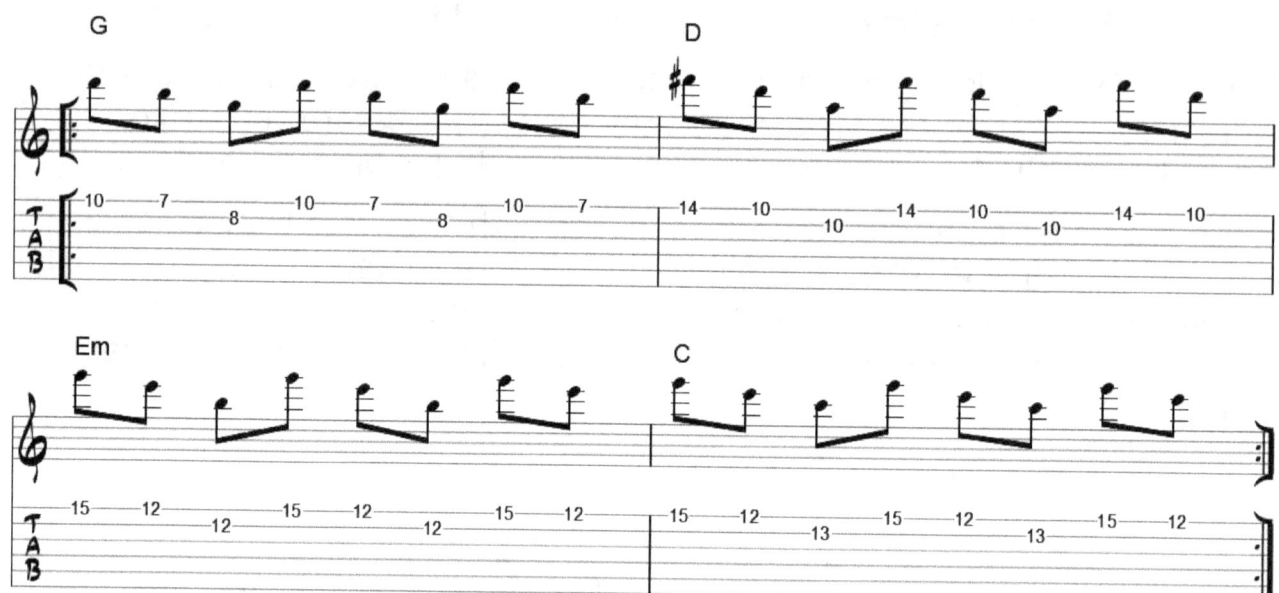

Here is the G D Em C progression with a small sweep shape in 8ths notes for the first three beats of the bar and then the arpeggio once as 16th note triplets on beat four.

SUMMARY

We are musicians and we are guitar players.

Music is Melody, Harmony, and Rhythm.

We think like a musician first and then go to our instrument.

We must always know the chords in our heads as we play.

Know the ROOT, THIRD and FIFTH of chords, as musicians and as guitar players. Start with the most commonly used chords: G C D Em and Am. (Remember the toggle switch for Major and minor doubles this.)

Knowing the OCTAVE SHAPES on guitar is crucial to understanding your fretboard.

ABOVE, ACROSS AND BEHIND is one of the cleanest ways to look at arpeggios on the guitar neck, especially when you see them in any of your MODE patterns.

GUIDE TONES are one of the secrets of sounding great. They bridge the typical scale solo sound with the arpeggio sound allowing you to "play the changes" and create a foundation for your melody/solo.

CHORD INVERSIONS are the gateways between rhythm guitar and lead guitar. They allow chords to move in different directions and show you the chord tones.

CAGED system is a guitar convention for the 5 shapes on our fretboard. For arpeggios we just need to focus on E C A shapes to get the 3 notes and inversions.

SECOND INVERSION ARPEGGIOS are a great compliment to the ROOT position arpeggios for our solos.

CHAPTER 9

TUNE IN

"I am a musician and a guitar player. Music is my language and my guitar is my voice. Music is Melody, Harmony and Rhythm. I develop my language skills and my instrument skills. They are two separate worlds working together to complete the circle of music."

Rhythm is the number one factor to sounding great as a musician.

WARM UP

Muted String Ladder (MSL) 6 strings 4 gears ONE PLUCK PER STRING (OPPS)

EXERCISE

Chord Inversions with GBE string shapes ascending and descending in Key of G. ROOT is on the High E String.

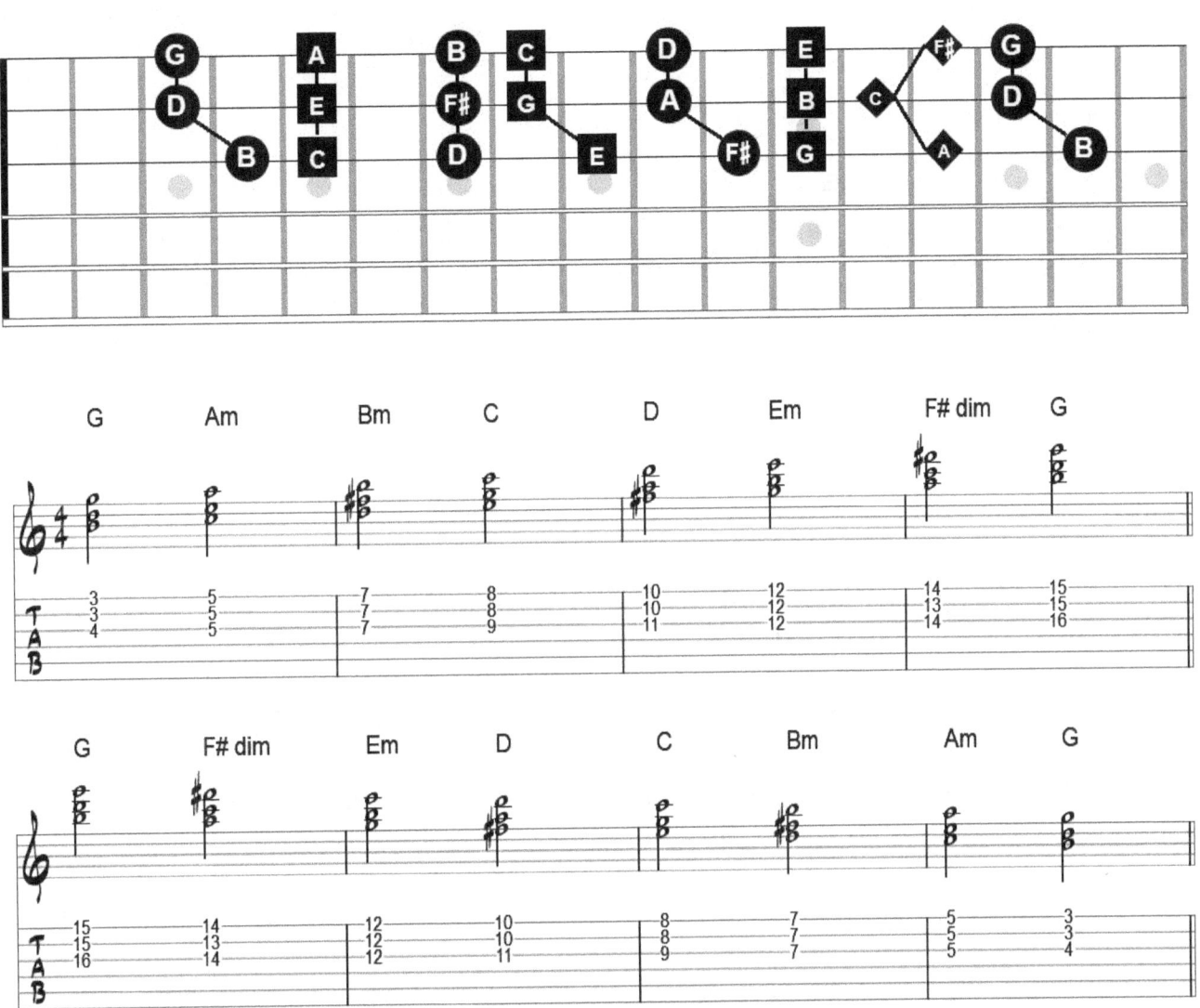

You can play the Em and F#dim chords in the open position as well. The Em is all open strings. The same shapes are at the 12th fret.

ACROSS Arpeggios in the Key of G *(Navigate the ROOT note on the B string)*

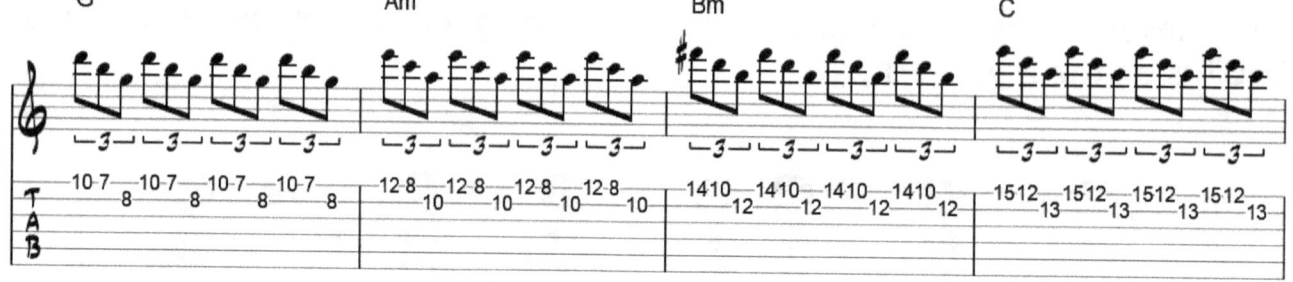

REVIEW

Let's take a look at a few examples of the different ways we can use arpeggios with another common chord progression:

I V vi IV in the **Key of A: A E F#m D**

Here is the progression using a repeated Tresillo (332) using 2nd INVERSION arpeggios shapes and ACROSS shapes.

Here is the same progression as chord inversions in position on the GBE strings and then on the DGB strings. They are simply written as quarter-notes but can be played in any way. Be creative.

GBE strings

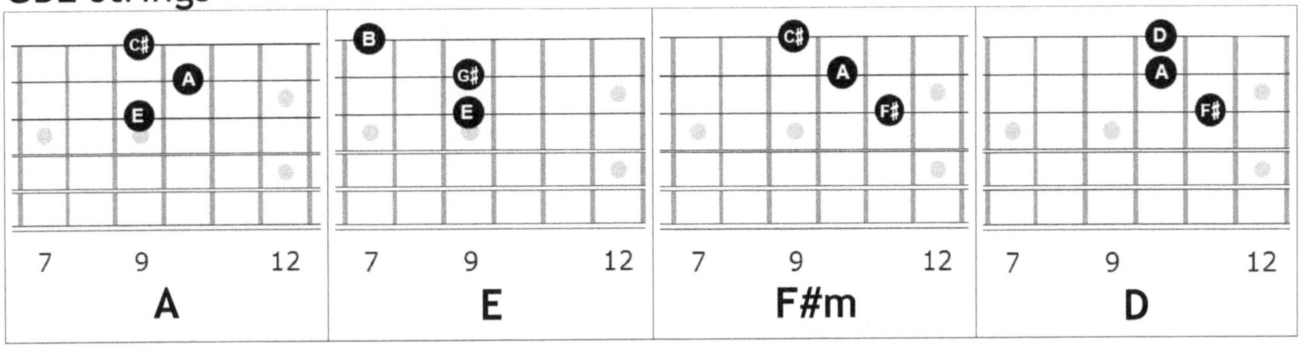

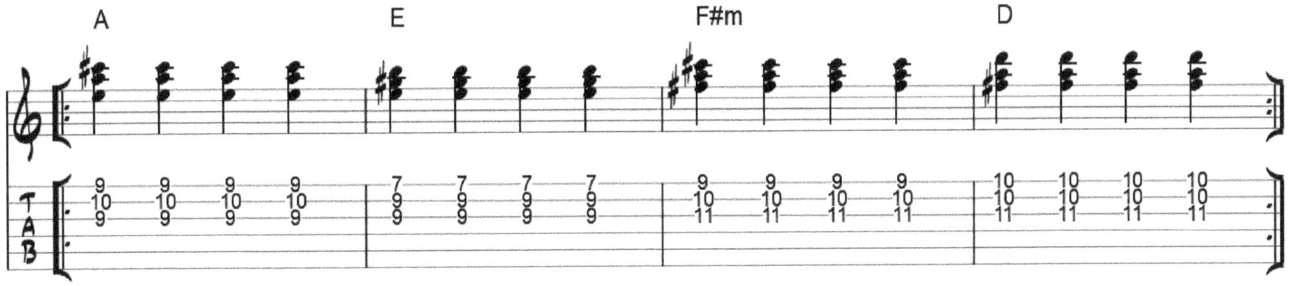

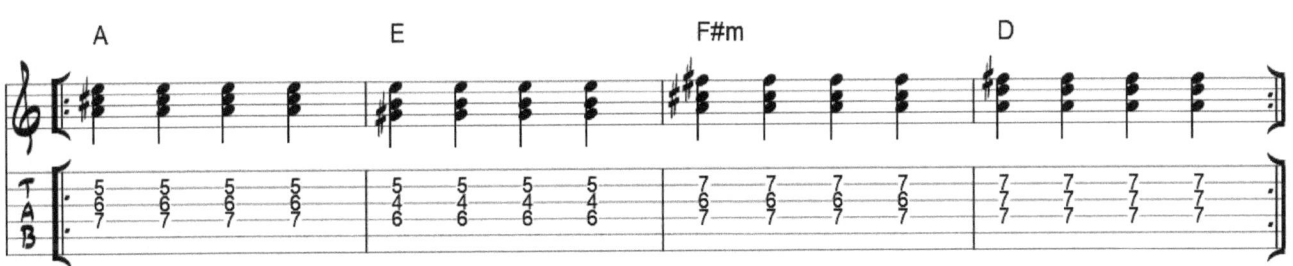

DGB strings

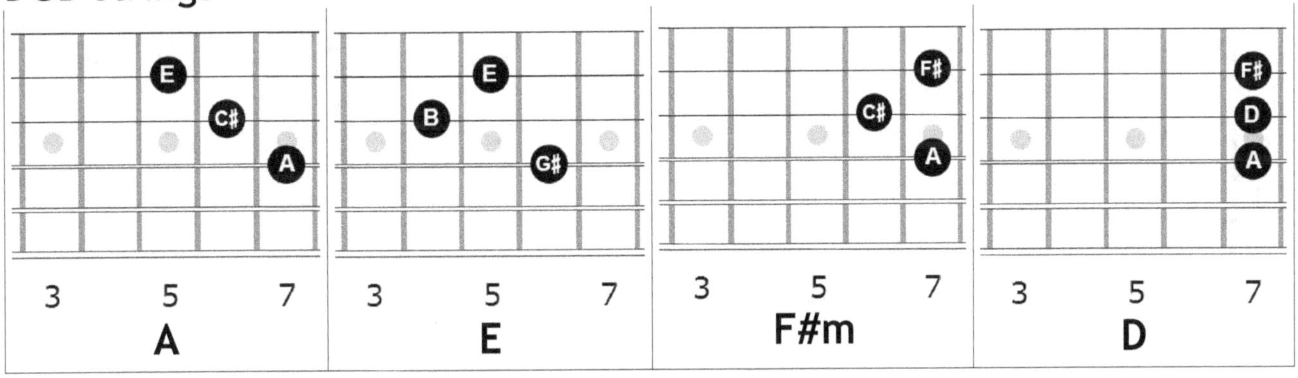

Here is the same chord progression with a Guide Tone Line and then an example using that line. Remember that the Guide Tone Line is made of chord tones that move a half or whole step (*it can be bigger*) to the next available chord tone. Each Chord tone in the guide tone line is either the root, the 3rd, the 5th and even the 7th of the chord in the progression.

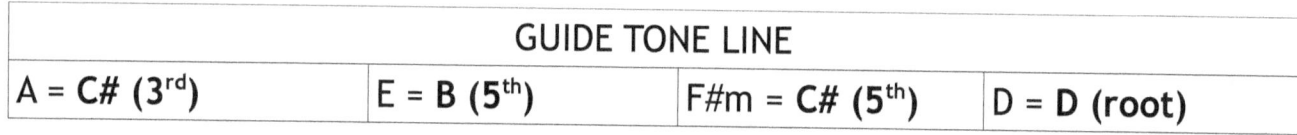

GUIDE TONE LINE			
A = C# (3rd)	E = B (5th)	F#m = C# (5th)	D = D (root)

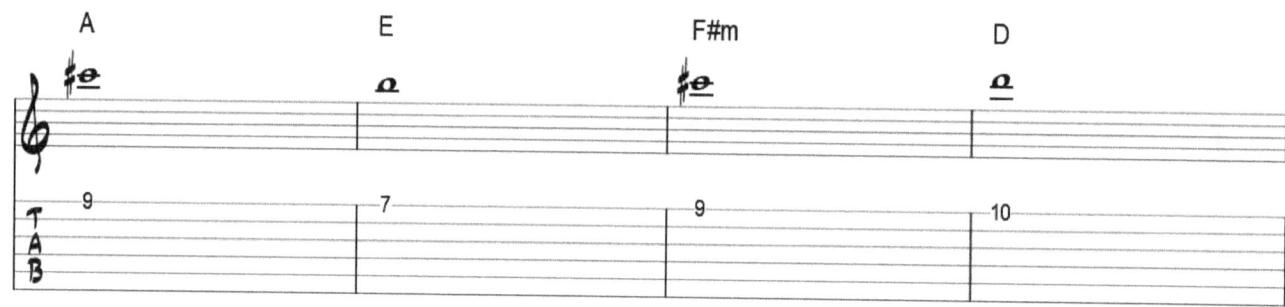

THIRDS and SIXTHS

When we started building arpeggios in the beginning of the book we looked at the important interval of a THIRD. The third is a distance between two notes. We note how important this interval is when it is from the ROOT to the THIRD of the chord (helps us determine anything Major or minor). The interval of a THIRD also happens between the 3rd and the 5th of the chord. Eventually you will see that it is also between the 5th and 7th of chords.

There are two types, MAJOR THIRD and MINOR THIRD. In the ACROSS and BEHIND shapes these occur on adjacent strings resulting in a harmonic interval

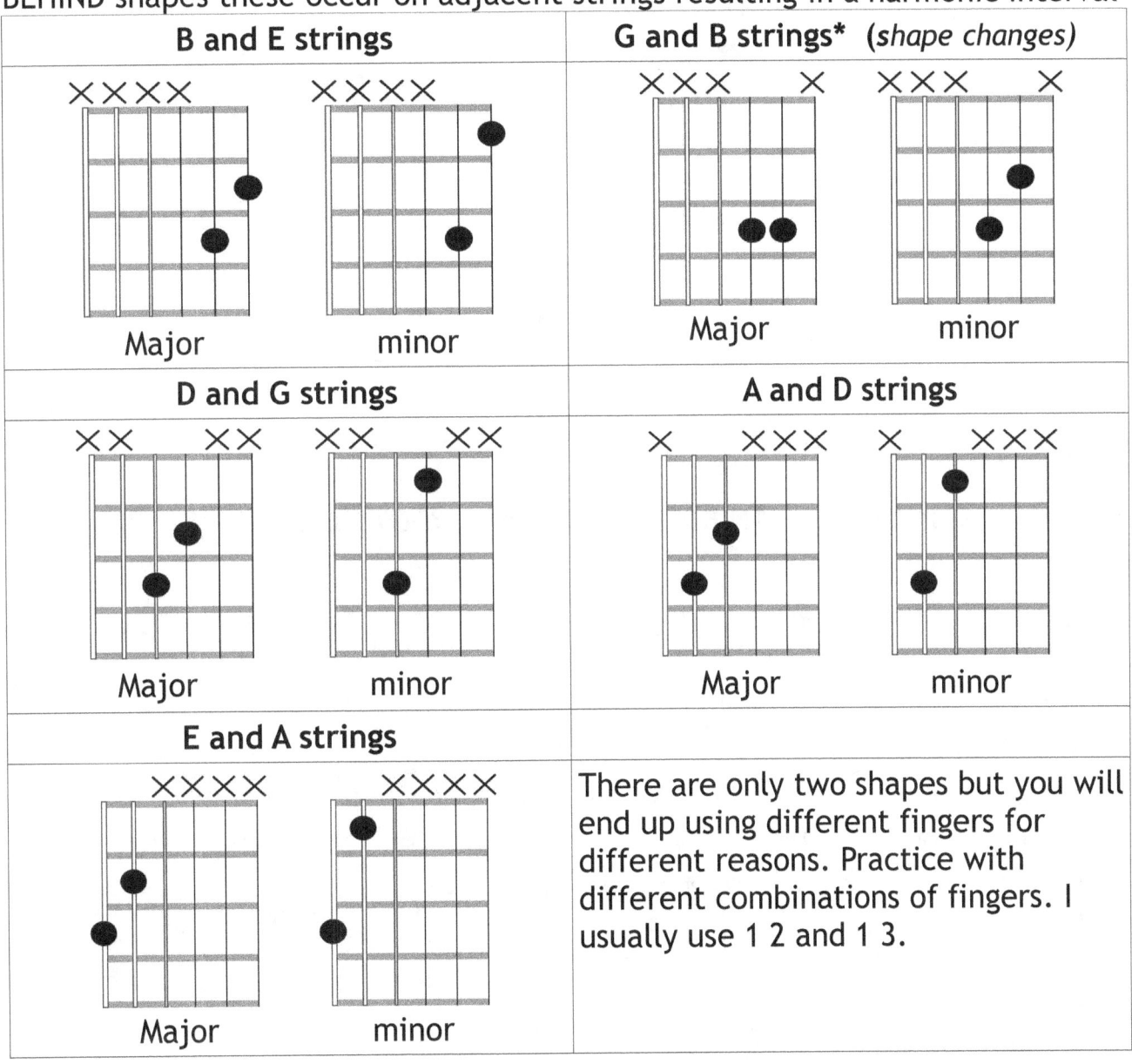

B and E strings	G and B strings* (shape changes)
Major minor	Major minor

D and G strings	A and D strings
Major minor	Major minor

E and A strings	
Major minor	There are only two shapes but you will end up using different fingers for different reasons. Practice with different combinations of fingers. I usually use 1 2 and 1 3.

There are only two shapes of thirds for every pair of strings and they are the same on all pairs of strings *except* the GB pair of strings (due to the B string only being tuned to a Major Third instead of a Perfect Fourth like the rest of the strings).

Usually when you play THIRDS you will use the note on the thicker of the string pairs to be the ROOT. In this diagram G is the ROOT. In the big picture it could be more than that. The G and B could be the minor THIRD and FIFTH of an E minor chord. It could even be the FIFTH and SEVENTH of a C Maj7 chord.

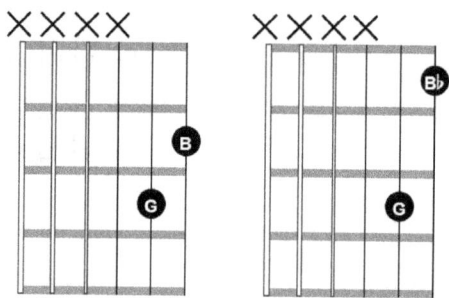

The Key of G in DIATONIC THIRDS on BE strings (*ROOT on B string*)

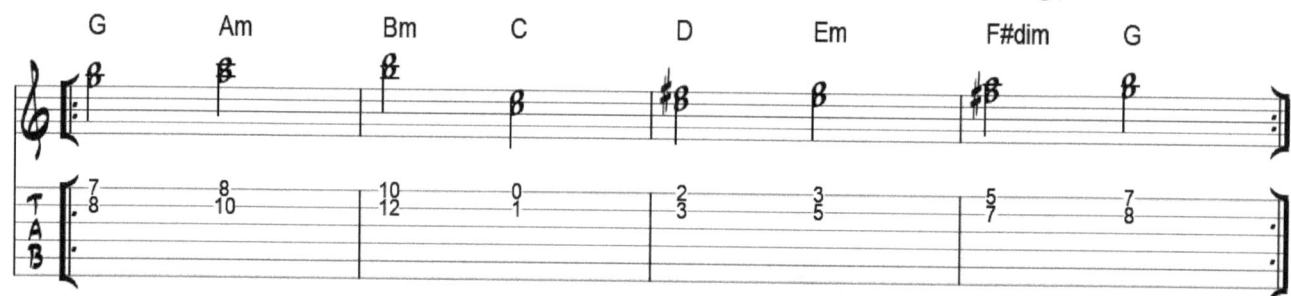

The Key of G in DIATONIC THIRDS on GB strings (*ROOT on G string*)

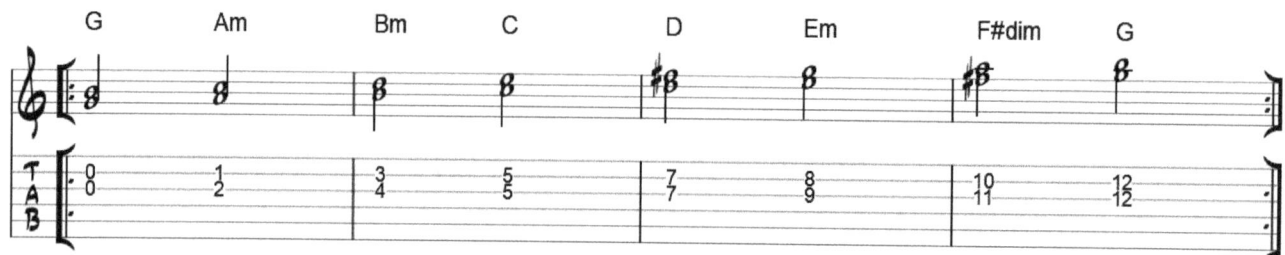

The Key of G in DIATONIC THIRDS on DG strings (*ROOT on D string*)

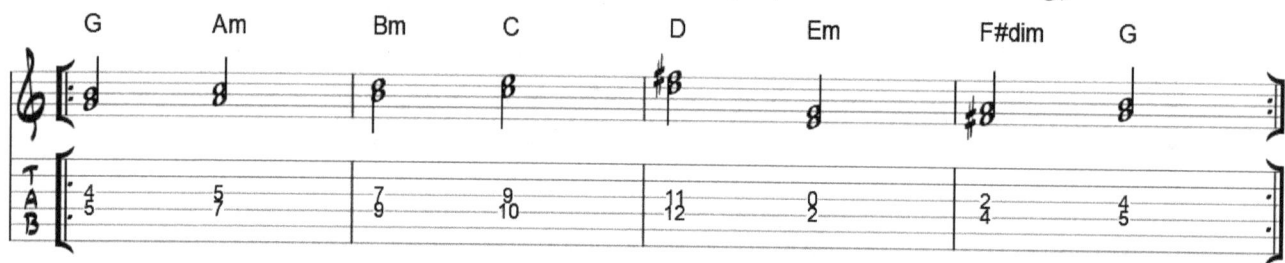

Intervals are the distance between the degrees of the scale.

In a G major scale G A B C D E F# G, there is a THIRD between the <u>G</u> and the <u>B</u>. and also between every other note.

THIRDS and SIXTHS are complimentary intervals. This means when you drop the B note and OCTAVE it is now a SIXTH away from the G (<u>B</u> C D E F# <u>G</u>). You can see it in the diagram below. Just like THIRDS there are Major and minor 6th intervals.

THIRD TO A SIXTH

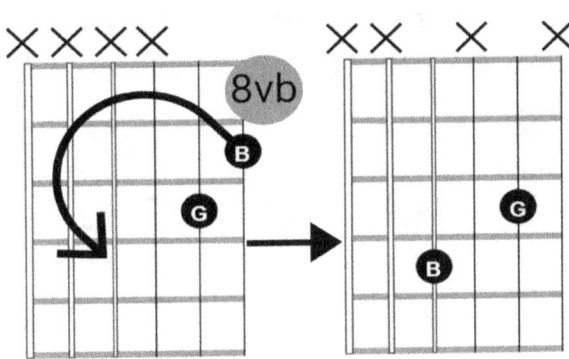

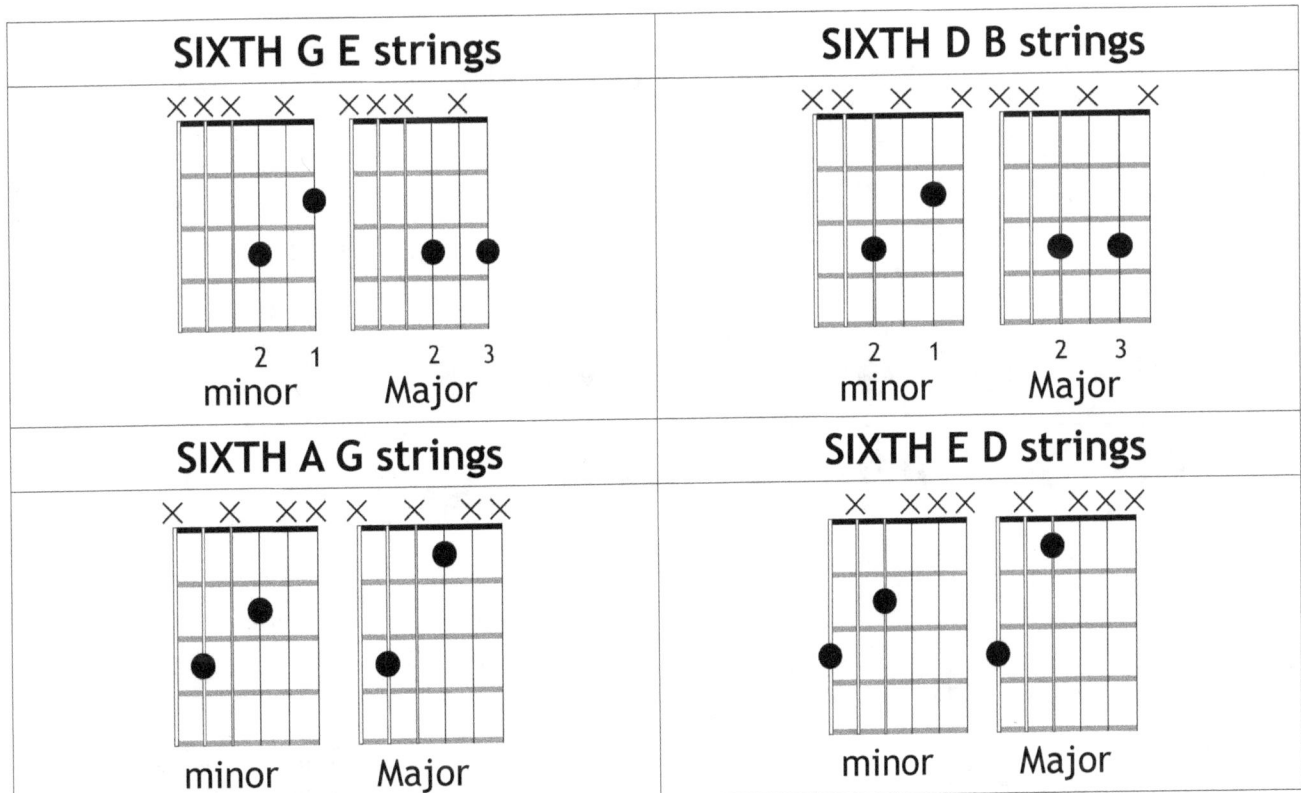

On the thicker strings fingerings will vary depending on situation.

When playing sixths on the highest pairs of strings you will always keep your middle finger on the lower string of the SIXTH and flip between first finger and ring finger on the higher string for other note in the SIXTH.

When we navigate the SIXTH it usually sounds best to keep the ROOT as the highest note (unlike the THIRDS). This gives it a really nice sound that compliments the chord. BUT, as in the second example, you can use the THIRD and FIFTH of the chord. (They make a SIXTH too.)

You should recognize that the SIXTH is the OUTER TWO notes of an INVERSION shape.

When you strum the SIXTHS just mute the middle string with your fretboard hand. You can also pluck them individually or even use hybrid picking.

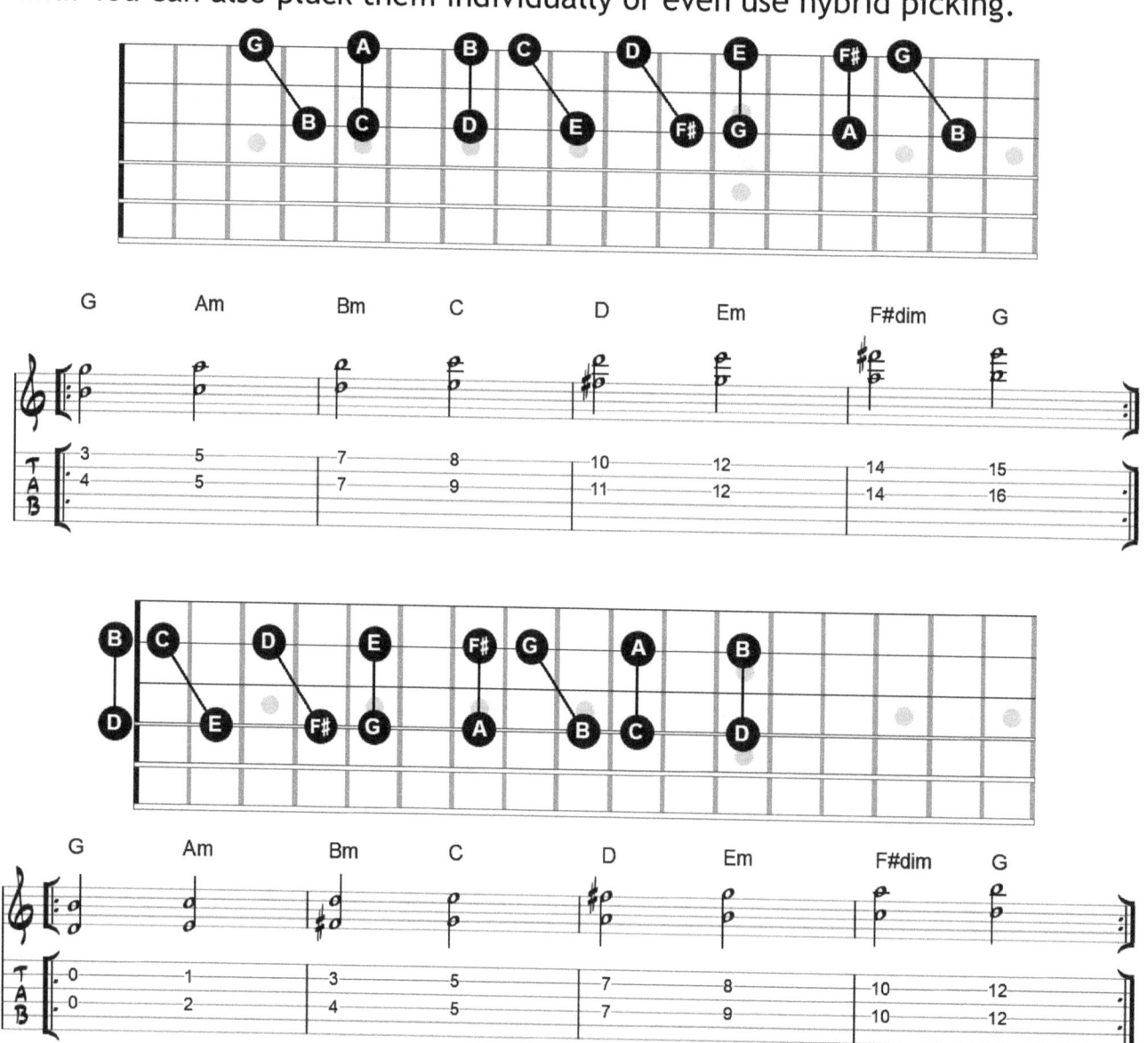

1 2 3 THIRDS and SIXTHS

With SIXTHS or THIRDS you can apply the 1 2 3 concept from the first chapter, using the ROOT, 2nd and THIRD. It works for THIRDS and SIXTHS too. You can see that the shape that is three away is part of the same first chord. If the first is GB (ROOT and THIRD) of a G chord, the shape three away is the BD and you can think of that as part of a B minor chord (ROOT and minor THIRD); BUT ALSO, as a G chord it is the THIRD and FIFTH of the chord. This means you can do three consecutive THIRDS or SIXTHS from a chord and you will get chord tones with a couple of passing tones to connect them.

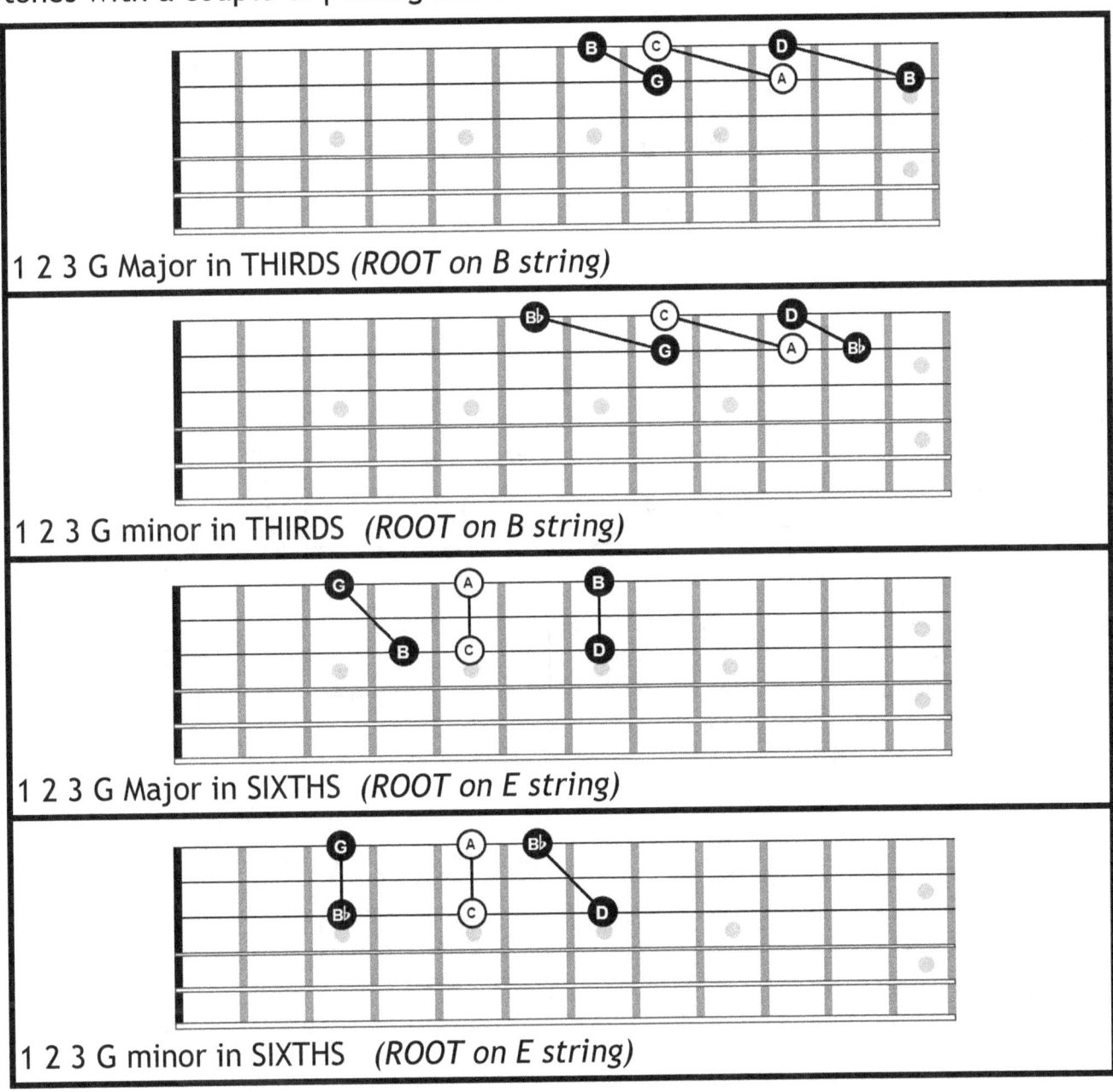

1 2 3 G Major in THIRDS *(ROOT on B string)*

1 2 3 G minor in THIRDS *(ROOT on B string)*

1 2 3 G Major in SIXTHS *(ROOT on E string)*

1 2 3 G minor in SIXTHS   *(ROOT on E string)*

PRACTICE

1 2 3 in THIRDS G D Em C

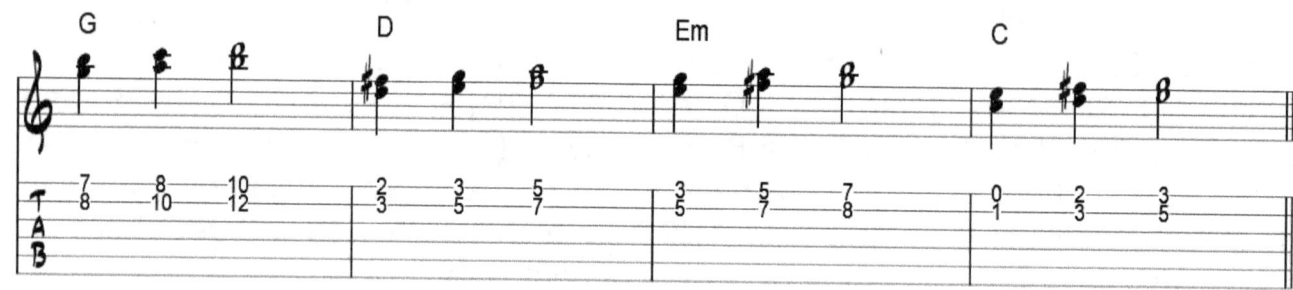

1 2 3 in SIXTHS G D Em C

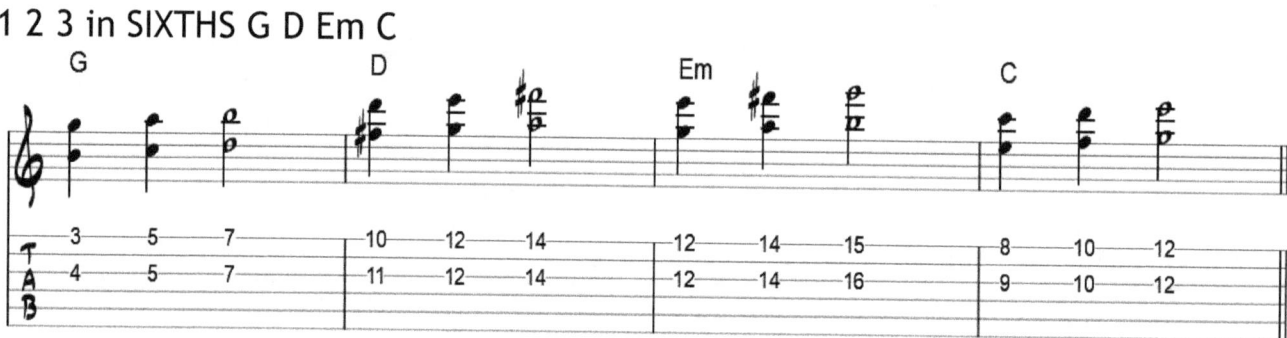

1 2 3 in THIRDS A E F#m D

1 2 3 in SIXTHS A E F#m D

SUMMARY

We are musicians and we are guitar players.

Music is Melody, Harmony, and Rhythm.

We think like a musician first and then go to our instrument.

We must always know the chords in our heads as we play.

Know the ROOT, THIRD and FIFTH of chords, as musicians and as guitar players. Start with the most commonly used chords: G C D Em and Am (remember the toggle switch doubles this.)

Knowing the OCTAVE SHAPES on guitar is crucial to understanding your fretboard.

ABOVE, ACROSS AND BEHIND is one of the cleanest ways to look at arpeggios on the guitar neck, especially when you see them in any of your MODE patterns.

GUIDE TONES are one of the secrets of sounding great. They bridge the typical scale solo sound with the arpeggio sound allowing you to "play the changes" and create a foundation for your melody/solo.

CHORD INVERSIONS are the gateways between rhythm guitar and lead guitar. They allow chords to move in different directions and show you the chord tones.

CAGED system is a guitar convention for the 5 shapes on our fretboard. For arpeggios we just need to focus on ECA shapes to get the 3 notes and inversions.

SECOND INVERSION ARPEGGIOS are a great compliment to the ROOT position arpeggios for our solos.

THIRDS and SIXTHS are great way to play double-stops on the guitar. They sound really rich and warm as they are part of the chords. They are great for rhythm guitar as well as in solos.

CHAPTER 10

TUNE IN

How many notes are in all of the chords in all of music? How many Major triads are there? How many minor triads? How many notes are in all of the scales in all keys and modes in music? How many notes have I ever listened to in all the music in my life? Twelve, there are only twelve notes in all of music for anything you have ever heard or ever plan on playing. Get to know the notes. They are with you without an instrument, so you can always think about them.

A, A#/Bb, B, C, C#/Db, D, D#/Eb, E, F, F#/Gb, G, G#/Ab

WARM UP

Muted String Ladder   6 strings 4 gears   ONE PLUCK PER STRING (OPPS)
Alternate Pick or economy pick

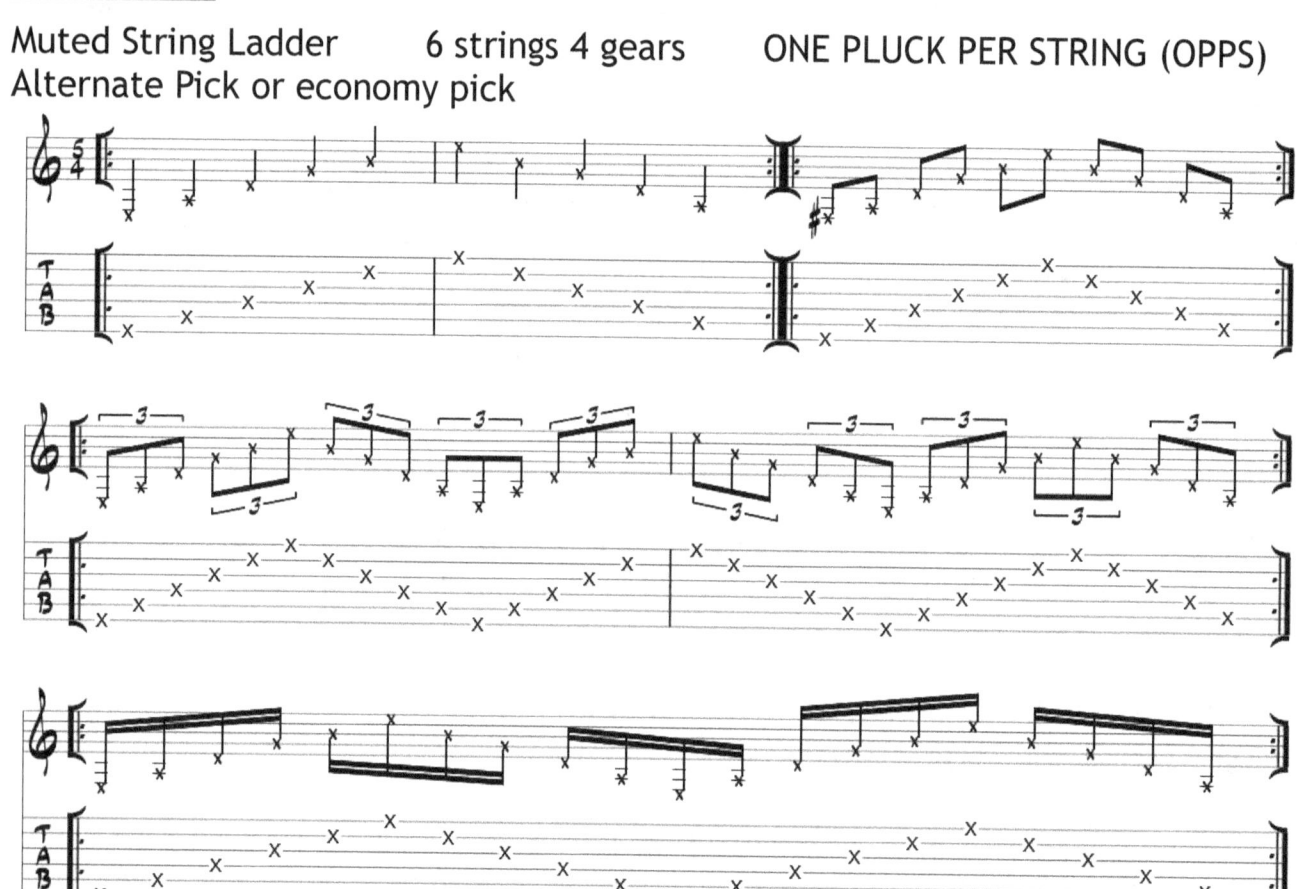

EXERCISE

Chord Inversions on the DGB strings in the Key of G.

G Am Bm C D Em F#dim

Play them as chords but also play them as individual notes. Do not hold the chord shape and arpeggiate. Think of it like your voice, one note-at-a-time.

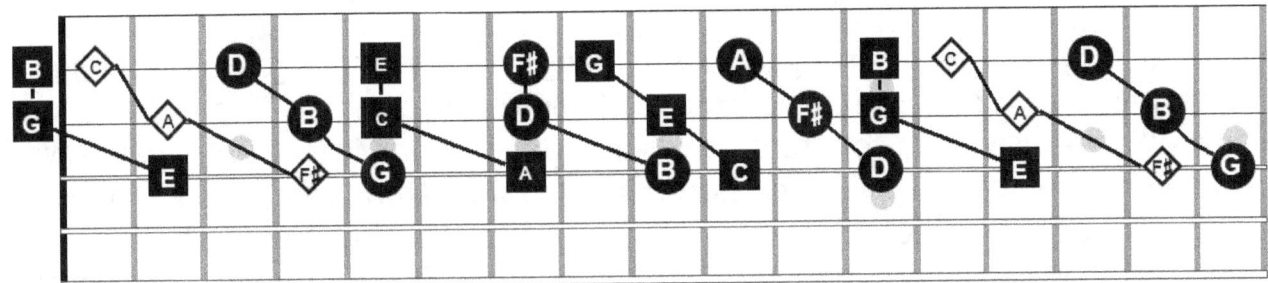

SHELLS

Take any arpeggio shape and treat it like a SHELL shape. Play the notes in the same order both directions. Reverse the order and do it again. Either play up and down a set of strings, or in position, at angles. Pick a rhythm and a starting point. It's a great way to get used to the tricky way in which we need to play arpeggios.

REVIEW

We first talked about how arpeggios exist in two basic ways, polyphonic and monophonic. Polyphonic methods are usually used to play chords, not with strums but with individual plucks of the notes in the chord and they all ring together. Monophonic arpeggios are more for melodic ideas, melodies, solos and when repeated almost act like polyphonic arpeggios. They are still one note-at-a-time, just like the voice.

As guitar players we use arpeggios in so many ways. We arpeggiate chords in a polyphonic way for songs (think "House of the Rising Sun" or "Stairway to Heaven"). We use them for solos as monophonic sounds in multiple ways. We can repeat the arpeggios of the chords in our solos (think second solo in "Hotel California" or the end of "Sultans of Swing"). We also use them in a monophonic way as guide tones (the notes of a chord used to "stitch" together a line that closely connects the chord tones of the progression). (Think first solo in "Hotel California," or even the hook of "Something" by The Beatles.)

As always, and more than ever we have to think like a musician and think like a guitar player recognizing they are two different skill sets. One is the language of music and one is an instrument that translates peoples feelings into sound.

Always be a musician first and guitar player second. Ask yourself what you need musically first. (What are the chords? What are the notes in the chords?) Then be a guitar player. (Is that an open chord or bar? Where can I play my G B and D notes on my instrument?)

As a musician, knowing arpeggios can help in so many ways. It can help you make a melody, play a solo, arrange background vocals to writing for strings and orchestra. Knowing the notes of the chords is getting right to the source of the sound. It's not really thinking keys or modes, but just the literal notes in the chords.

As a guitar player, knowing the arpeggios will most likely benefit your ability to phrase. Even when playing a pentatonic solo, if you pay careful consideration to the chords, you will bend the right note to match the chord and release the bend to a note that matches the next chord. Jimi Hendrix and especially David Gilmour are very good at this.

Here are some of the main ideas we covered as
musicians and guitar players.

Think and know the chords
Always keep track of the chords as you play them. Know the notes of each
chord and the other tones that surround it. Use your inner voice to call out
every chord to yourself as it goes by.

Melodic bass lines
The first step to playing arpeggios is establishing the ROOT note for each
chord on the downbeat of the change. Play this on the top (high sounding)
strings as we want it to be a melody. It should act like a bass line by landing
the ROOT on the first beat of the change.

Third on same string -1 2 3
Once you get the ROOT note you can locate its THIRD on the same string. It's
above it on the same string by either 3 frets (minor 3rd) or 4 frets (Major 3rd).
The THIRD is the "TOGGLE" switch in music for anything Major and minor.
1 2 3 refers to the idea of Do Re Me which is the ROOT, 2nd and 3rd of a Major
scale (2 whole steps each). You can always get this sound once you find a
ROOT. You would only do a Whole-step and then half-step for the minor third.
Such a simple idea and sound can go a really long way and sound so good.

R 3 5 on one string
We learned that triads are either a Major third followed by a minor third
(for Major Triad) or minor third followed by a Major third (for minor triads).
You should now navigate those on every single string. Imagine that any single
triad exists every 12 frets on a single string. You have six strings, there is a full
triad on all six strings of every triad in existence! That's incredible!, When I
took lessons with Mike Stern he would have me do just that for all triads and
seventh chords for all keys.

Above Across and Behind
Above, Across, and Behind is a simple way to look at any arpeggio starting on
any note of the guitar. It helps better navigate the three notes of a triad on
the fun house mirror that the guitar is. Once you realize the triad only has
three combinations when played beyond one string it becomes easier to
conceptualize the nature of the guitar fretboard.

Guide Tones

Guide Tones are the chord tones that guide you through the chord progression. You start with a chord tone of the first chord and move to a chord tone of the next chord, usually with the smallest interval available. You continue this through the whole progression. These lines form what I think of as a fence post. They just form a very simple path that establishes the chords. You can build on it for solos, use it for background vocals or strings. They are bass lines and melodies. You can figure out guide tones ahead of time, or when you get comfortable, you can improvise them.

ECA for Chord Inversions

Considering the CAGED system we saw that you only need to focus on the E C and A shapes of a bar chord to find the inversions for the triads. By taking any consecutive three strings you will get the inversions from each bar shape. The harmonic arpeggios are equally at home as chords for rhythm playing and for tracing and landing on for soloing. We looked at the shapes on the GBE string group and the next DGB string group. You can also find these on the ADG, and EAD string groups too.

ECA Shapes for Above Across and Behind, and scale patterns

Once we learned how to extract chord inversions from the E, C, and A shapes we learned how to relate the pentatonic patterns to the chord shapes. We also looked at the two octave arpeggios that happen inside each of the E, C, and A shapes.

Thirds and Sixths with 1 2 3

Using our knowledge of the inversions we can take two of the notes and make thirds and sixths. Both of these are wonderful as solo elements and rhythmic elements. So many guitar players use them in so many creative ways. Listen to Steve Cropper on "Sittin' On the Dock of the Bay" or "Soul Man." From Jim Croce and George Harrison to the Allman Brothers and Jimi Hendrix, guitar players always take advantage of these awesome sounds.

NECK ANATOMY ARPEGGIOS

First you must see the Short to Long Octaves.

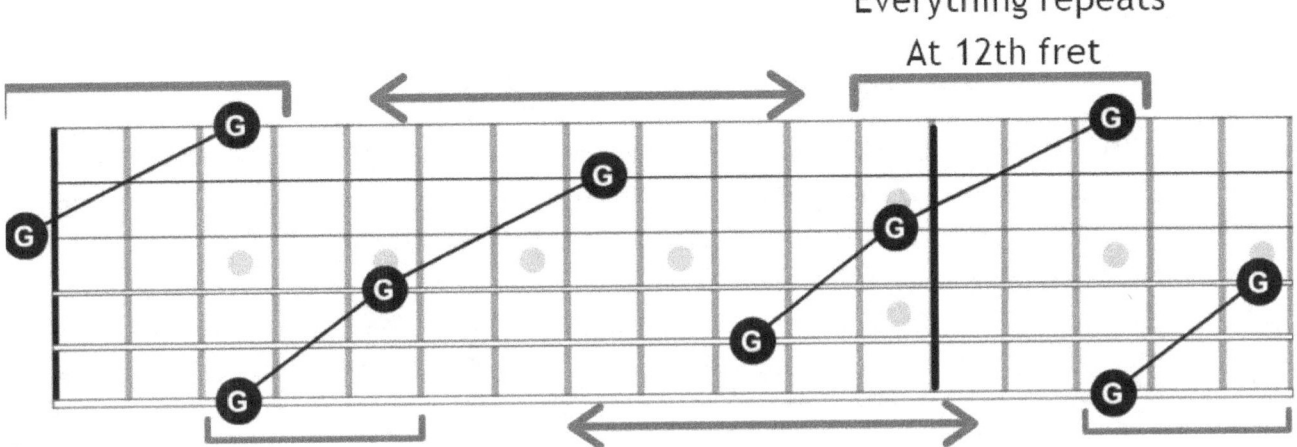

Everything repeats
At 12th fret

Then you can build arpeggios from each one.

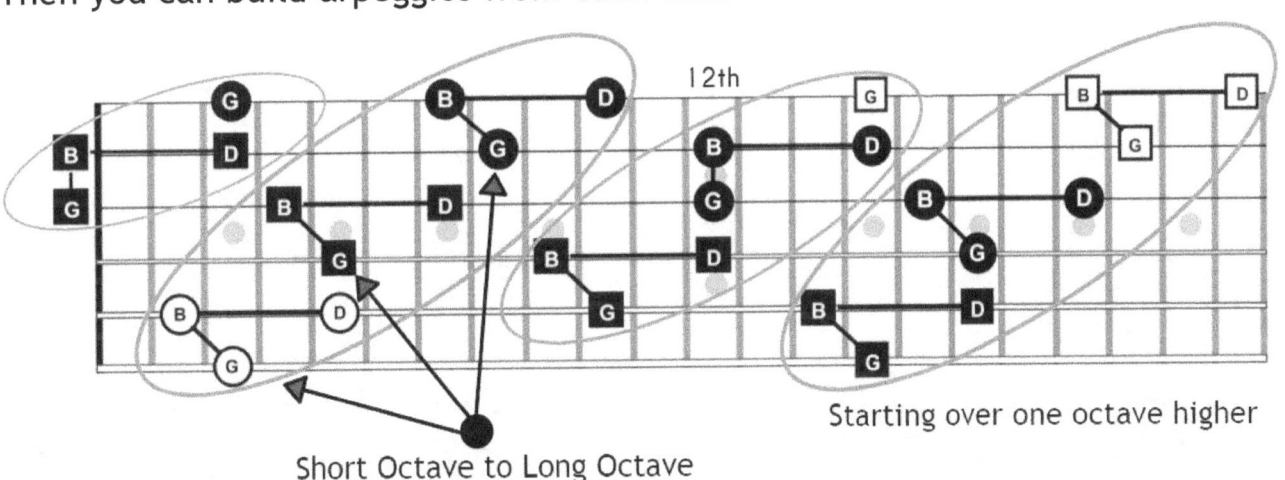

Short Octave to Long Octave

Starting over one octave higher

Different shape = different octave

You can see the E C and A shapes here too. All the notes, arpeggios, chords and scales are sitting on top of each other. It just depends on how and what you are looking for.

PRACTICE

Diatonic arpeggios are in the Key of G using the ACROSS shape for 3 octaves with Neck Anatomy. Navigate each ROOT note (G A B C D E F#) for 3 octaves using

SHORT OCTAVE to LONG OCTAVE.

Move your hand every three notes. Whenever you place your hand down you play the arpeggios and then quickly move your hand to the next octave. The speed happens between the movement of the hand.

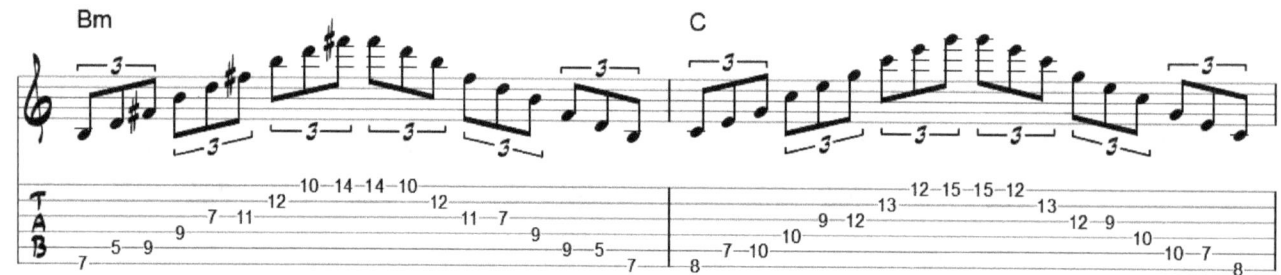

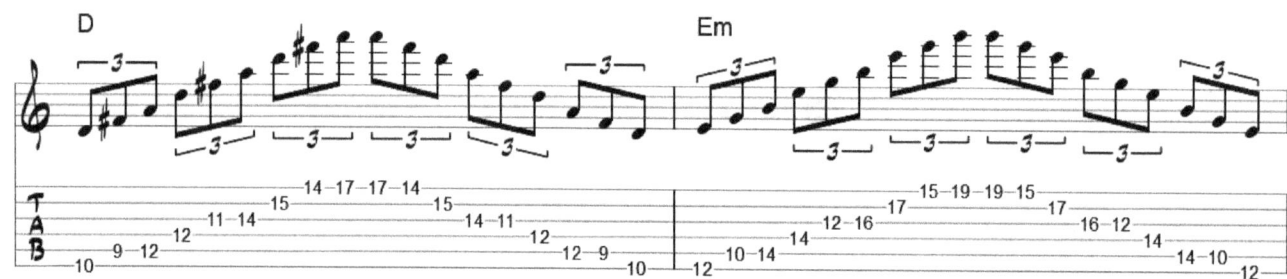

SUMMARY

As a Musician
- Know the 12 notes.
- Get to know the notes in chords starting with G, C, D, Em and Am.
- Learn the Thirds of all Major chords to turn them into minor chords.
- Music is Melody, Harmony and Rhythm.
- Rhythm is the most important element.
- Always keep the chords going in your head.

As a Guitar Player
- See the notes on the fretboard.
- See the THIRDS above the ROOT on any string.
- Be able to play any arpeggio on a single string.
- Be able to navigate the different shapes of arpeggios from a Root note (Above, Across, and Behind).
- Know the E C A Caged shapes and how to navigate them.
- Master the chord inversion shapes for the GBE and DGB strings.
- Use the inversion shapes to help with thirds and sixths.

We have to remember that all of the information we learned about Arpeggios was already in our scales and patterns. It's nothing new other than how we choose to look at the information we already have. Instead of seeing a scale as just a bunch of black dots, we can look at it as all of the arpeggios in the key.

We use Arpeggios to enhance our sound and add to our already existing database of information on how to solo. It's important to have all of your knowledge merge into a homogeneous approach. There are always notes, chords, keys, modes, arpeggios happening. There is always rhythm and almost always melody and harmony.

Learning music is a circular process and not a linear one. At a certain point you will not learn anything new in music. You will revisit and learn the same information deeper and quicker. Just like any language, at a certain point you don't learn many new words. You learn to speak more clearly and more eloquently. To be poetic you don't need more words, just better ideas to describe. Music is the same, and with an incredible sense of rhythm you will always sound good no matter what you know or don't know.

Keep moving on your path, and at the same time you will go back and revisit everything you have learned. This process happens indefinitely. If you ever pick up another instrument you will have a tremendous head start. Once you adapt to the physical instrument you will be playing music quickly.

Spend most of your time playing music and not practicing music. All of our heroes played, incessantly. You will improve when you play. You will play music better because you always play and not practice. Get better at playing music by playing music. You can't race a parked car. It needs to be in motion, pulling against gravity and centripetal forces to fully understand how to move.

Music is ALWAYS in time, no matter what. Therefore you should ALWAYS play music in time. Why would you not?

You can play music with no melody (chords only) and you can play music with no harmony/chords (vocal melody for example) but you CANNOT play music without RHTYHM. It is impossible. That's how important rhythm is. Every single note is a fast pulse of a wave, a rhythm. Every note is a rhythm! When I heard George Russell say that my mind was blown. It is all about rhythm.

"I am a musician and a guitar player. Music is my language and my guitar is my voice. Music is Melody, Harmony and Rhythm. I develop my language skills and my instrument skills. They are two separate worlds working together to complete the circle of music."

Rhythm is the number one factor to sounding great as a musician.

HOW TO PRACTICE

Tune in - 5%
Take a few minutes to clear your head. Turn off your devices and do what you need before you dig in and play. Remind yourself that you are a musician and a guitar player. Everything you play should be rhythmically based, always.

Warm up - 10%
Muted String Ladders, Shells, and Changing Gears are some of the best warm ups. They simply get your fingers, hands, and internal clock all synchronized. Muted String ladders focus on rhythm and pick control. Changing Gears really harnesses the ability to feel and play rhythms. The Shells are best of both worlds and are like "wax on, wax off." Practice real world moves and patterns.

Exercise - 15%
This is where you run scales and patterns. This is a great opportunity to play through the five patterns. Always play them in time and play them ascending and descending or as "Round the Block" zigzag the patterns.

Review - 15%
Just as important as learning something new, make sure you're understanding something you have recently learned. It's essential to build your growth by reviewing past topics and understanding them deeper.

New Topic - 15%
Learn something new. However easy or small, it is growth. Every little bit moves you towards your goal of sounding great as a musician. Maybe it's learning the names of the notes in a scale, or a lick, a chord, anything that helps you sound better. You can learn as a musician, as a guitar player, and as a rhythmist.

"Practice" - 40%
The best way to practice is not to practice, but to play! It's true. Every one of our heroes played music more than anything else. Practicing refers to some future date that you are preparing for. Playing is now. Play in time, carry the song, the beat, the groove, all of it. Self Generating is the best way to play and get your practicing in. If you are practicing a turnaround in a blues, then you play the 12 bar blues and at the end you play the turnaround. If you miss it, keep playing and get it the next time around. This is what you would do onstage. Keep playing and you will get better, as you would if you "practiced."

THOUGHTS

The learning path in music is circular. You will learn something and come back around to it and get to know it better. Every time you do this you will gain more confidence and experience. There is only so much actual information you will need to learn. It is all about how to use and manipulate that material that makes the magic of music start. Learning music is not a linear path but a circular one.

Music is Melody (notes), Harmony (chords), and Rhythm.
Rhythm is the number one factor to sounding great.

Where attention goes, energy flows. So much of being a better musician is all about your mind set and what you focus your time and energy on.

"The process of learning consists not in what is brought to the learner, but what is drawn out of him." (Plato)

"The Student as a boxer, not a fencer. The Fencer's weapon is picked up and put down again. The Boxer's is part of him, all he has to do is clench his fist." (Marcus Aurelius-Meditations)

"The Student as a musician, not a guitarist. The guitarist's instrument is picked up and put down. The musician's is part of him. All he has to do is tap, clap, and sing." (Suke Cerulo)

You can play music without melody (just chords) and you can play music without chords (just melody, like your voice), but you can *never* play music without rhythm, it's impossible. As soon as you tap your foot or pluck a note, rhythm happens.

The language of music hasn't really changed in hundreds of years. It is much older than the guitar. Once you know the language, that's it. Now you can learn as many instruments as you want. You just have to adapt to the physical part of the instrument.

The instrument is silent without you. You are music!

GLOSSARY

<u>Audiation</u> Inner Hearing but also the musical knowledge behind it, to hear the knowledge.

<u>Arpeggio</u> The notes of a chord played in succession rather than simultaneously.

<u>BPM</u> Beats-per-minute. How music tempo/beat/quarter-note is measured.

<u>Chord</u> Usually three or more notes played simultaneously.

<u>Chord Inversion</u> The notes of a chord rotating in order (example R35, 35R, 5R3).

<u>Chord Scale</u> The scale matched to a particular chord, using its chord tones and appropriate notes in between to best fit for playing the changes.

<u>Chord Tone</u> A single note, as part of a chord.

<u>Degree, Scale</u> The number in the scale at which a note lives. There are seven notes in the diatonic scale. They are numbered 1-7 for their degrees.

<u>Diatonic</u> meaning "of the key". Notes and chords only in that key.

<u>Diatonic Harmony</u> The seven chords that naturally occur in all keys and its resulting formula.   (I ii iii IV V vi viidim)

<u>Fingerpicking/Fingerstyle</u> Fingerpicking is using fingers only to pluck the strings on guitar. Fingerstyle might include thumb and/or fingerpicks.

<u>Gear</u> (LGW) Slang for describing the different rhythms. First gear is quarter-notes, second gear is eighth-notes; third gear is triplets; fourth gear is sixteenth-notes, and so on.

<u>Half-step</u> The smallest interval in music. It is one fret on a guitar, and a single piano key to the next (for example white to black)

Harmonic Rhythm The rhythmic pacing of chord changes; how often the chords change (for example every two beats versus every four beats).

Harmony Chords or notes being played simultaneously to produce a sonorous sound. Chord progressions and the underlying chord motion.

HO PO Short for Hammer-ons and Pull-offs

Hybrid Picking When you combine the use of a pick and the remaining three fingers to get a combination of flat pick and fingerstyle.

Inner Hearing Hearing music in your inner ear by memory even if you don't know it musically. (Happy Birthday, Hot Cross buns, and others)

Key One of 12 families built around the 7 note Major scale. Contains 7 chords, one for each of its own notes built by the Rule of Thirds.

Legato When a musician connects the notes of a phrase in a smooth and consistent sound without any silence in between the notes.

Lick A slang term used to describe a group of notes, usually used in a lead solo. These can be recognized by style, genre, person, and more.

LGW Lead Guitar Workshop

Melody One note-at-a-time succession of notes in a pleasing fashion. The signature of a song and the part that is copyright protected.

Mode A function of a scale/key. When a Key or scale is based on any one of its chords/notes. This changes the half-steps in relation to where they live in the scale, producing varying sounds of Major and minor chord progressions and scales.

Monophonic Producing one note-at-a-time only.

Muted String Ladder (MSL)(LGW) A picking hand exercise to improve rhythm and confidence in Down, Up, and Alternate picking across the strings

Musical Truth (LGW) A term to describe some of the fundamental rules in music that every musician follows regardless of instrument.

<u>Neck Anatomy</u> (LGW) Using octaves in a short to long connection to help navigate the fretboard and move around like other instruments do and not be tied to changing patterns. There are 2 pairs of "short to long" octaves (E and A string).

<u>Pentatonic</u> Meaning "five notes of the home." These are ancient five note scales believed to have originated in Asia. There are two main types, Major and minor, and they are in all types of music all around the planet.

<u>Playing the changes</u> A slang term a musician uses when they change their note choices/scales/arpeggios to match each individual chord instead of a "Global" sound of playing one scale for all the chords.

<u>Polyphonic</u> The ability to play multiple notes simultaneously. Pianos and guitars are polyphonic, the human voice is not.

<u>Riff</u> A slang term for rhythm guitar part made up of notes instead of chords. Think "Heartbreaker" by Led Zeppelin, "Crazy Train" by Ozzy.

<u>Rhythm</u> The pulse in music. The basis for everything music. The measured beat and its subdivisions.

<u>Root</u> The "main" note in a Key/chord/scale/arpeggio. The one everything else revolves around. The sound that comes home resolves to the Root.

<u>Root Position</u> When a scale pattern, arpeggio, or chord shape has its ROOT as the lowest note.

<u>Rule of Thirds</u> Stacking every other note in a scale to create a chord. Three notes for a triad and four notes for a seventh chord.

<u>Self-Gen</u> (LGW) Using your inner ear and inner clock to start and play music yourself, in time, especially with consideration of switching between chords and soloing.

<u>Shell</u> (LGW) A hand dexterity exercise to help overcome any guitar playing issue. It involves a fingering, a performance method, and rhythm.

Staccato Each note is sharply detached or separated from the others.

Tied In music notation when an arch connects two or more rhythms to create a sustained sound. Especially useful to achieve lengths of time not possible with traditional rhythms (for example a note that last 1 ½ quarter notes.)

Tonic The "main" note/chord. Often the key but not always. It is the note/chord that everything else resolves to.

Tresillo A Latin based rhythmic figure where 8 eighth-notes are grouped in 3 3 2 notes to total 8.

Triad A three note chord. Usually achieved by stacking every other note in a scale for a total of three notes.

Voice Leading A term used for connecting the chord tones of one chord to another with the notes moving the least amount necessary to make the chord change. This makes a really smooth sound.

Whole-step The second smallest interval in music. It is two half-steps in distance. Most scales consist of half-steps and whole-steps.

ABOUT AUTHOR

Michael Cerulo (aka Suke) is a guitarist and multi-instrumentalist whose life long love and devotion to music has given him a very distinct and identifiable sound. Whether it's his fluid guitar melodies, the warm organic tone of his flute, or his own recordings where he plays and produces all of the music, Suke's individuality, creativity and talent are evident in all of his creations.

Born in a suburb of Boston, Suke was raised in a musical family. His grandfather (George Lane) was a composer, multi-instrumentalist and bandleader during the late 40's and early 50's. All four of George's siblings were musicians as well, often being employed in his big band. The youngest brother helped start **Berklee College of Music**. Suke began playing guitar and taking music lessons when he was twelve. Being persistent, with an unbending intent to learn and grow, he then enrolled in Berklee College of Music in Boston. After graduating in '94, while also working for MOTU music software, Suke became a full time touring musician. Suke composed, played guitar and flute with his band **Schleigho.**

Schleigho (pronounced shlay-ho) was formed at Berklee in 1993 and was touring around the country a year later. The band's style is a mix of jazz and funk, with each of its four members contributing equally to bring about an unprecedented wall of sound. Being predominately instrumental, the band's incredible talent and versatility allows them to go from opening for the Allman Brothers to playing high scale jazz venues while satisfying the most discriminating of tastes. The band released their first CD (*self-titled*) in 1995, '*Farewell to the Sun*' in 1997 and '*In the Interest of Time*' in 1998. In 2000 the band signed with **Flying Frog Records (owned and managed by members of the Allman Brothers)**. Under Flying Frog Records they released '*Continent*' in 2000, and '*Live at HoDown 2000*' the following year. Schleigho has met with great success over the years; from amassing a substantial and dedicated national following to '*Continent*' breaking into the top 20 on CMJ and college Jazz radio charts. Averaging over 200 shows annually across the country, they have shared the stage with **The Allman Brothers band, Derek Trucks, Bela Fleck, John Scofield, Karl Denson, Maceo Parker, G. Love and Special Sauce, Galactic, moe. and Soulive**, to name a few. Schleigho has performed at the JVC Jazz festival (NYC), the Gathering of the Vibes, the High Sierra Music Festival, and the Berkshire Music Festival, among others, and are veterans of the club/college circuit and large festival scene for over 20 years.

Suke also performed for years with the band **Conehead Buddha**, which is a song structured improvisational fusion of hip-hop, rock, and jazz, flirting with many styles from drum and bass to latin and reggae. It's a high energy show featuring Terence and Shannon Lynch.

Another avenue he has been steadily involved with is the production of music for multimedia. For the last twenty years Suke has been developing his production and engineering abilities in his own project studio to further enhance his musical visions. He created *Tone Over Tone* in which he composes, performs, engineers, mix's and masters recordings to be licensed for multimedia applications. This area of music production allows for infinite amounts of creation and timbre. Using conventional instruments, modern technology and a thorough musical background, Suke now creates breathtaking music that utilizes almost any instrument in creation with lush sound design.

His sound is refreshing and his performance is intense. You can always hear diverse musical influences throughout his compositions and soloing. Music from the likes of Jimi Hendrix and Van Halen to John Coltrane, Roland Kirk, and George Benson. From Jeff Beck and Ozzy to Herbie Hancock, Mingus and Miles. From Igor Stravinsky to Square Pusher and Amon Tobin.

Suke currently resides in New York City with his family and has been the *Director of Lead Guitar Program at New York City's "Best" Guitar School* since 2004. He has taught over 15,000 lessons and classes amassing a staggering amount of teaching experience. Suke is also responsible for the musical evaluations of incoming teachers and has often taught the other teachers at the school. The hundreds of students and thousands of hours teaching have help sculpt and mold the success of his teaching methods.

Whether it's playing in a group context, performing, teaching or creating and producing music, Suke always incorporates a fine balance of taste and technique with a result that's not soon forgotten. He always keeps his eye and ear to the future while respectfully paying homage to his influences and tradition.